Taxcafe.co.uk Tax Guides

Salary versus Dividends

& Other Tax Efficient
Profit Extraction Strategies

Nick Braun PhD

Important Legal Notices:

Published by:
Taxcafe UK Limited
67 Milton Road
Kirkcaldy KY1 1TL
Tel: (0044) 01592 560081
Email: team@taxcafe.co.uk

ISBN 978-1-911020-17-2

17th edition, May 2017

Disclaimer
Before reading or relying on the content of this tax guide please read the disclaimer.

Disclaimer

1. This guide is intended as **general guidance** only and does NOT constitute accountancy, tax, investment or other professional advice.

2. The author and Taxcafe UK Limited make no representations or warranties with respect to the accuracy or completeness of this publication and cannot accept any responsibility or liability for any loss or risk, personal or otherwise, which may arise, directly or indirectly, from reliance on information contained in this publication.

3. Please note that tax legislation, the law and practices of Government and regulatory authorities (e.g. HM Revenue & Customs) are constantly changing. We therefore recommend that for accountancy, tax, investment or other professional advice, you consult a suitably qualified accountant, tax advisor, financial adviser, or other professional adviser.

4. Please also note that your personal circumstances may vary from the general examples provided in this guide and your professional adviser will be able to provide specific advice based on your personal circumstances.

5. This guide covers UK taxation only and any references to 'tax' or 'taxation', unless the contrary is expressly stated, refer to UK taxation only. Please note that references to the 'UK' do not include the Channel Islands or the Isle of Man. Foreign tax implications are beyond the scope of this guide.

6. All persons described in the examples in this guide are entirely fictional. Any similarities to actual persons, living or dead, or to fictional characters created by any other author, are entirely coincidental.

About the Author & Taxcafe

Dr Nick Braun founded Taxcafe in 1999, along with his partner Aileen Smith. As the driving force behind the company, their aim is to provide affordable plain-English tax information for private individuals, business owners and professional advisors.

Over the past 17 years Taxcafe has become one of the best-known tax publishers in the UK and has won several prestigious business awards.

Nick has been a specialist tax writer since 1989, first in South Africa, where he edited the monthly *Tax Breaks* publication, and since 1999 in the UK, where he has authored several tax books including *Landlord Interest, Small Business Tax Saving Tactics* and *Pension Magic*.

Nick also has a PhD in economics from the University of Glasgow, where he was awarded the prestigious William Glen scholarship and later became a Research Fellow.

Contents

Introduction

This guide answers the most common question asked by company owners: "What's the best way to take money out of my company if I want to pay less tax?"

In Part 1 we kick off with a plain English guide to how companies are taxed. We explain how corporation tax is calculated and why companies are such powerful tax shelters.

We then explain how company owners are taxed. As a director/shareholder you can choose the best *mix* of salary and dividends. We examine the pros and cons of each type of income.

Company owners can also choose the most tax efficient *level* of income. We explain how by smoothing your income, or varying it significantly from year to year, you may be able to reduce your tax bill considerably.

New Tax Rules for Dividends

The tax treatment of dividends has completely changed with effect from 6 April 2016. Dividend tax credits have been abolished so tax calculations are now a lot simpler. Unfortunately, however, new dividend tax rates have been introduced that are 7.5% higher than the previous ones.

In this part of the guide, using lots of examples, we explain how much tax you will pay on your dividend income under the new rules.

In Part 2 we reveal how much tax-free salary and dividend income you can withdraw from your company during the current tax year. You'll discover how to calculate the "optimal" tax–free salary and how couples in business together can pay themselves £33,000 tax-free this year.

In Part 3 we explain how much dividend income you can take taxed at just 7.5% and how to avoid paying tax at 32.5%.

This part of the guide also contains important tax saving strategies for parents who want to avoid the child benefit tax charge.

This kicks in when your income exceeds £50,000 but many company owners will be able to avoid it completely or in part.

There is also important tax planning information for high income earners (those with income over £100,000 or £150,000).

In Part 4 we turn to company owners who have significant amounts of income from other sources (e.g. rental income, other business income and investment income). We explain why you may need to adjust your company salary or dividends to avoid the higher tax rates that kick in when your income reaches certain key thresholds (£45,000, £50,000, £100,000 and £150,000).

We also examine some tax planning techniques that can be used to reduce or eliminate the tax payable on your other income.

Part 5 explains how company owners can gift shares in the business to their spouses, partners or children and save up to £12,487 in tax this year, with similar savings every year. We also show how additional savings can be achieved by paying tax-free salaries to family members (including minor children) and the traps you must avoid when splitting income with other people.

Part 6 looks at alternative profit extraction strategies:

- **Directors' loans** – How they can be used to avoid or postpone tax.

- **Rent** – Why getting your company to pay you rent is now more tax efficient than a dividend in many circumstances.

- **Interest** – How to receive up to £6,000 of tax-free interest.

- **Pension contributions** – Why they're better than dividends, who should make them (you or the company), plus a new chapter on putting property into a pension.

- **Company Cars, Vans & Motoring Costs** – a Plain English guide to the tax rules.

- **Mobile Phones** – Getting your company to pay the cost.

- **Capital gains tax** – How to pay 10% tax when you sell or wind up your company.

In Part 7 we turn to some of the practical issues and dangers that may be experienced when extracting money from your company, including:

- How to avoid the minimum wage regulations

- How to make sure your salary is a tax deductible expense

- Making sure your company has sufficient distributable profits to declare dividends

- How to declare dividends properly and avoid an HMRC challenge

- The circumstances in which HMRC may try to tax your dividends as earnings

In Part 8 we show how company owners, by altering the amount of income they withdraw from their companies, can reduce the amount of capital gains tax payable when assets like rental properties are sold.

Finally, the last chapter of the guide explains how you may be able to completely avoid tax by emigrating, including details of the new statutory residence test.

Using This Guide & Limitations

This tax guide deals primarily with the 2017/18 tax year which started on 6 April 2017 and finishes on 5 April 2018.

There are references to other tax years, for example when discussing the advantages and disadvantages of postponing income to a future tax year.

However, it is important to emphasise that the tax rates and tax laws that will apply in future tax years are not known with any degree of certainty.

Tax rates and tax laws (including HMRC's interpretation of those laws) are continually changing. The reader must bear this in mind when reading this guide.

Please note that, although owners of small trading companies are this book's main target audience, this is NOT supposed to be a do-it-yourself (DIY) tax planning guide.

My purpose in writing this guide is to explain in plain English how companies and company owners are taxed and provide some tax planning ideas that can be taken to an accountant or other professional advisor for further discussion.

I do not recommend 'going it alone' when it comes to this type tax planning and there are several reasons for my cautious approach.

Firstly, although the guide covers a fair amount of ground, it does not cover every possible scenario – that would be impossible without making the guide much longer and possibly much more difficult to digest.

In other words, in places I have had to sacrifice definitiveness in favour of making the guide a manageable and hopefully enjoyable read for the average small company owner.

Companies come in many different shapes and sizes, as do their owners, so it is possible that the information contained in this guide will not be relevant to your circumstances.

In particular, please note that this guide is aimed mainly at UK resident director/shareholders who own and work for UK resident companies.

Secondly, the main focus of this tax guide is *income tax* planning: helping company owners pay less tax on their salaries and dividends. There are, however, other taxes that often have to be considered, including capital gains tax and inheritance tax.

Steps that you take to reduce one type of tax can have an adverse impact on your liability to pay other taxes. While some mention is made of other taxes in this guide, I cannot guarantee that all interactions are covered.

Thirdly, there are potential risks involved when it comes to structuring your affairs to reduce the tax payable on salaries, dividends and other payments made by your company.

While most of the tax planning ideas contained in this book are widely used by many accountants and other professional advisers, and have been for many years, this does not mean they have the blessing of HM Revenue & Customs!

There are lots of grey areas when it comes to this area of tax planning and there are no guaranteed tax savings.

In other words, we cannot be certain that some of the tax planning ideas contained in this book will not be subject to some sort of attack from HMRC, even if only at some point in the future.

For example, in the chapters that follow we will show that the most tax-efficient mix of income for most company owners is a small salary coupled with a larger dividend. While this may be the *mathematically* optimal income mix for many company owners, the tax savings are not guaranteed.

There is a danger that HMRC will seek to tax dividends as earnings in some circumstances and may frown on any reduction in an existing salary – see Chapters 35 and 36 for more information.

Fourthly, there are also *non-tax* factors that have to be considered when deciding how much money you withdraw from your company and in what form. In some instances other considerations will outweigh any potential tax savings.

For all of these reasons it is vital that you obtain professional advice before taking any action based on information contained in this guide. The author and Taxcafe UK Ltd cannot accept any responsibility for any loss which may arise as a consequence of any action taken, or any decision to refrain from taking action, as a result of reading this guide

The General Anti-Abuse Rule

A new general anti-abuse rule (GAAR) came into operation on 17 July 2013.

Tax arrangements are "abusive" if they cannot reasonably be regarded as a reasonable course of action – this is commonly referred to as the double reasonableness test.

Clearly it's very subjective and HMRC has sought to reassure taxpayers that there will be a "high threshold" for showing that tax arrangements are abusive:

"In respect of any particular arrangement there might be a range of views as to whether it was a reasonable course of action: it is possible that there could be a reasonably held view that the tax arrangements were a reasonable course of action, and also a reasonably held view that the arrangement is not a reasonable course of action. In such circumstances the tax arrangements will not be abusive for the purposes of the GAAR."

An indicator that tax arrangements may not be abusive is if they were "established practice" when entered into and HMRC indicated its acceptance of that practice at the time.

Tax arrangements may be abusive if, for example, the tax result is different to the real economic result, for example tax deductions or tax losses that are significantly greater than actual expenses or real economic losses.

If you think that all of the above is a bit vague and subjective, you are not alone. Even the best tax brains in the land don't know what this test means in practice. When legislation contains words like "reasonable" and "abusive" you know you have to be on your guard!

The question being asked by some tax advisers is this: will the anti-abuse rule be used to attack the sort of 'normal' or 'mainstream' tax planning carried out by thousands of small company owners, for example taking small salaries and dividends?

Many tax experts believe that well-established, conventional tax planning will not be attacked by HMRC using the GAAR. Instead the focus will be on the extreme end, for example 'aggressive' or 'artificial' tax avoidance schemes.

This view seems to be backed up by HMRC guidance published in January 2015 which says the following about small company dividends:

"Just as it is essential to understand what the GAAR is targeted at, so it is equally essential to understand what it is not targeted at. To take an obvious example, a taxpayer deciding to carry on a trade can do so either as a sole trader or through a limited company whose shares he or she owns and where he or she works as an employee. Such a choice is completely outside the target area of the GAAR, and once such a company starts to earn profits a decision to accumulate most of the profits to be paid out in the future by way of dividend, rather than immediately paying a larger salary, is again something that should in any normal trading circumstances be outside the target area of the GAAR."

Nevertheless, at present the simple truth is that no one knows how HMRC will apply the general anti-abuse rule to company owners in the years ahead and whether it will eventually affect certain tax planning practices that many regard as mainstream, including some of those contained in this guide.

Part 1

How Companies & Company Owners Are Taxed

Chapter 1

How Companies Are Taxed

Companies generally pay corporation tax on both their income and capital gains.

For the current financial year, which started on 1 April 2017, all companies (except some in the oil and gas sector) pay corporation tax at the same flat rate of 19%.

The rate was previously 20%.

Things weren't always this simple. There used to be two headline corporation tax rates: a higher rate for companies with profits over £1.5 million (known as the 'main rate') and a lower rate for companies with profits under £300,000 (the 'small profits rate').

There was also a third rate applying to profits between £300,000 and £1.5 million.

Not only has corporation tax become a lot simpler, it has also been significantly reduced, as the Government has tried to boost the UK as a business destination. Back in 2007 the main rate was 30%.

Smaller companies haven't enjoyed such significant tax cuts, although it must be remembered that the small profits rate was due to rise to 22% back in 2011.

Both big and small companies do, however, benefit from the latest cut in the corporation tax rate from 20% to 19% on 1 April 2017.

The rate will be cut again to 17% on 1 April 2020.

In their 2017 election manifesto the Conservatives reaffirmed that this cut will take place: *"we will stick to that plan, because it will help to bring huge investment and many thousands of jobs to the UK"*.

Most small company owners will welcome these cuts because they will partly offset increases in the tax paid on the dividends they withdraw from their companies.

Northern Ireland

In Northern Ireland the rate is expected to be cut to 12.5% when corporation tax powers are devolved to the Northern Ireland Assembly, possibly as soon as April 2018.

This would bring Northern Irish companies in line with those in the Republic, making Northern Ireland a tax haven within the UK.

Don't take my word for it. Even Ballymena's most famous son, Hollywood actor Liam Neeson, is excited: "I firmly believe that the commitment of the Northern Ireland Executive to reduce the rate of corporation tax to 12.5% from April 2018 really is a potential game-changer for our economy."

Before corporation tax can be devolved, however, Northern Ireland has to demonstrate to the UK Treasury that its finances are on a stable footing. Following the uncertainty caused by the collapse of the Northern Irish Government, April 2018 is looking much less like a done deal.

So which companies/activities will qualify for the special tax rate when it is introduced?

The special corporation tax rate will apply to *trading profits* only. Other types of income, including investment income and property rental income, will be subject to the UK main rate of corporation tax, as will capital gains.

Micro, small or medium-sized enterprises (SMEs) will pay tax at the special rate on all their trading profits if they qualify as a 'Northern Ireland employer', i.e. if at least 75% of their staff time and costs relate to work carried out in Northern Ireland.

SMEs are currently defined under EU regulations as businesses with fewer than 250 employees and turnover of less than €50 million or a balance sheet total of less than €43 million.

Larger companies, with activity in both Northern Ireland and the rest of the UK, will have to treat their Northern Ireland trading activity as if it were a separate business and allocate profits appropriately. The special rate will apply to profits that relate to the Northern Ireland trading presence, defined as a 'Northern

Ireland regional establishment' (generally speaking a fixed place of business).

Legislation is being introduced to allow SMEs which do not qualify as Northern Irish employers, but do have a Northern Ireland regional establishment, to elect to use the large company rules to identify profits to which the Northern Irish tax rate applies. Otherwise they would not be able to benefit from the Northern Irish rate.

Look through Taxation Quashed

Throughout 2016 the Orwellian "Office of Tax Simplification" (OTS) investigated a system of "look through" taxation for certain small companies.

A look through system, if made compulsory, would take away the tax benefits of using a company.

Under look through taxation, instead of paying corporation tax, the affected company owners would pay income tax and national insurance on all the profits of the business, just like sole traders and partnerships do.

As we shall see, the advantage of using a company is that you can smooth your income and control your income tax bill by paying yourself dividends as and when you like.

Furthermore, those who wish to grow their businesses or protect themselves from a downturn can retain profits inside the company, in which case the only tax payable is 19% corporation tax (falling to 17% in 2020).

Fortunately, the OTS has decided not to recommend look through taxation because it would not simplify the tax system and would harm investment. So, hopefully, at least for now, this specific threat has gone away.

Multiple Companies

Business owners used to be punished for owning more than one company. This is no longer the case (since April 2015).

What happened was the £300,000 small profit band (where the lower corporation tax rate was payable) had to be divided up among 'associated companies'.

For example, in the case of two companies, each company would start paying corporation tax at the higher rate when its profits exceeded £150,000 (instead of £300,000).

The associated company rules prevented the profits of one business being artificially spread over more than one company to avoid the higher rates of corporation tax.

The associated company rules have become largely redundant with the introduction of the single flat rate of corporation tax for all companies.

Nowadays you aren't penalised for owning more than one company – they all pay tax at the same rate (currently 19%).

There are many reasons why you may wish to own more than one company. For example, someone who owns an ecommerce business and a restaurant chain may wish to keep them separate so that each company can be sold more easily in the future.

Someone who owns a software company and a property rental business may wish to keep them in separate companies so that the 'trading' business (the software company) is not contaminated by the 'non-trading' business (the property rental business).

Companies that own too many non-trading assets, like rental property, can lose important tax reliefs, including Entrepreneurs Relief, Holdover Relief and Business Property Relief.

Example
Maz owns an insurance broker called Insure Clever Ltd. The company makes profits of £200,000 per year. Maz recently inherited £500,000 and decides to buy some rental properties. He works out that he will be better off investing through a company instead of personally and sets up a second company called Clever Property Ltd (see the Taxcafe guide

Using a Property Company to Save Tax *for a full discussion of this topic).*

Before April 2015, Maz would have been penalized for owning two companies. Insure Clever Ltd's small profit band would have been reduced from £300,000 to £150,000 and the company would have paid corporation tax at the higher rate on £50,000 of its profits.

But if instead Maz decided to stick with one company and use Insure Clever to buy the properties, it's possible he would have lost his entitlement to various tax reliefs like Entrepreneurs Relief.

Now, however, Maz can keep his insurance and rental property interests separate without suffering a higher corporation tax bill. Both companies will pay 19% tax on all their profits.

Although the associated company rules are no longer relevant when it comes to determining the corporation tax rate your companies pay, they're still relevant for other purposes, for example in deciding whether a company has to pay corporation tax in quarterly instalments. Instalments are generally payable by companies whose profits exceed £1.5 million but this amount is divided up if there are any associated companies.

Whereas small companies currently only have to pay their corporation tax nine months after the financial year has ended, companies subject to instalments have to start paying tax half way through the year.

The associated company rules have also been simplified with effect from 1 April 2015. From this date a new '51% group test' applies. For example, if a company owns 51% of the share capital of three subsidiaries, all four companies will be associated. The £1.5 million profit limit would then be divided by four to determine whether each company has to pay corporation tax in instalments.

In the past the fact that Maz owns 100% of both Insure Clever Ltd and Clever Property Ltd would have meant that the companies were associated. However, under the new rules the fact that the ownership link is an individual doesn't count, i.e. the companies are not associated.

So some companies which previously were subject to the quarterly instalment regime may now find themselves outside it.

Trading Companies vs Investment Companies

In tax jargon a 'trading' company is one involved in, for want of a better word, 'regular' business activities, e.g. a company that sells goods online, a catering company or a firm of garden landscapers.

Common types of *non-trading* company include those that hold substantial investments in property or financial securities or earn substantial royalty income.

Corporation Tax

A few years ago, if your company was engaged mainly in non-trading activities it would have been punished with a higher corporation tax rate.

This is because a company classed as a close investment holding company (CIC) was not able to benefit from the small profits rate. It was forced to pay corporation tax at the main rate on all of its profits.

For example, if you set up a company to buy and sell stock market shares, a few years ago it would have been taxed at 30% (the main rate of corporation tax), even if it only made a small amount of profit.

Companies that own rental property were always excluded from the CIC provisions and were allowed to enjoy the small profits rate.

All this is no longer relevant because since April 2015 all companies, both trading companies and investment companies, pay corporation tax at the same flat rate, currently 19%.

Capital Gains Tax

If a company has too many non-trading activities (including most property investment and property letting) it may lose its trading status for capital gains tax purposes.

This will result in the loss of two important CGT reliefs:

- Entrepreneurs Relief
- Holdover Relief

Entrepreneurs Relief allows you to pay capital gains tax at just 10% (instead of 20%) when you sell your company or wind it up.

Holdover Relief allows you to give shares in the business to your children, common-law spouse and other individuals and postpone CGT. (You don't need Holdover Relief to transfer shares to your spouse because such transfers are always exempt.)

A company will only lose its trading status for CGT purposes if it has 'substantial' non-trading activities. Unfortunately to HMRC 'substantial' means as little as 20% of various measures such as:

- Assets
- Turnover
- Expenses
- Profits
- Directors' and employees' time

HMRC may attempt to apply the 20% rule to *any* of the above measures.

Inheritance Tax

Shares in trading companies generally qualify for business property relief which means they can be passed on free from inheritance tax. However, if the company holds investments (including rental property) this could result in the loss of business property relief.

The qualification criteria are, however, more generous than for CGT purposes and a company generally only loses its trading status for inheritance tax purposes if it is 'wholly or mainly' involved in investment related activities.

To be on the safe side you may want to ensure that the company's qualifying activities exceed 50% of each of the measures listed above (e.g. turnover, time, profits etc).

For more information see our guide *How to Save Inheritance Tax.*

Accounting Periods vs Financial Years

A company's own tax year (also known as its 'accounting period') may end on any date, for example 31 December, 31 March etc.

Corporation tax, on the other hand, is calculated according to financial years. Financial years run from 1 April to 31 March. The 2017 financial year is the year starting on 1 April 2017 and ending on 31 March 2018.

This matters when it comes to calculating how much tax your company will pay if the corporation tax rate has changed.

For example, on 1 April 2017 the corporation tax rate fell from 20% to 19%. A company whose accounting period runs from January 2017 to December 2017 will therefore pay corporation tax as follows:

- 3 months to 31 March 2017   20%
- 9 months to 31 December 2017   19%

The practical effect is that the company will pay 20% corporation tax on approximately one quarter of its profits and 19% tax on three quarters of its profits. (It doesn't matter at what point during the financial year the profits are actually made.) This means the company's *effective* corporation tax rate will be 19.25%.

A company whose accounting period runs from 1 August 2016 to 31 July 2017 will pay corporation tax as follows:

- 8 months to 31 March 2017   20%
- 4 months to 31 July 2017   19%

Thus the company will pay 20% corporation tax on two thirds of its profits and 19% tax on one third of its profits. This means the company's *effective* corporation tax rate will be 19.66%.

A company whose accounting period runs from 1 April 2017 to 31 March 2018 will simply pay 19% corporation tax on all of its profits.

Please note, in most of the corporation tax calculations in this guide we use the current headline 19% rate, for example when calculating the corporation tax relief on salaries or company pension contributions. This is to keep things simple.

However, if your company's current accounting period started before April 2017, it will have a slightly higher effective corporation tax rate.

For example, a company whose current accounting period runs from January to December 2017 will enjoy £192.50 corporation tax relief (19.25%) for every £1,000 it spends on things like salaries before 31 December 2017. Spending after this date will attract just £190 corporation tax relief (19%).

A company whose accounting period runs from 1 August 2016 to 31 July 2017 will enjoy £196.60 corporation tax relief for every £1,000 it spends before 31 July 2017. Spending after this date will attract just £190 of corporation tax relief.

The amounts involved are not significant and probably won't affect your decision making much.

Making Tax Digital

Under Making Tax Digital (MTD) businesses and landlords will be required to use commercial accounting software and update HMRC quarterly.

VAT reporting commences from 1 April 2019 and corporation tax reporting commences from 1 April 2020.

Spreadsheets will be permitted as an appropriate form of digital record-keeping, provided the business owner has suitable software which interfaces with the spreadsheet to make the appropriate quarterly submission.

Companies as Tax Shelters

This guide shows company owners how to extract money from their companies in the most tax efficient manner possible. However, before progressing to the various profit extraction strategies it is worth reiterating why it may be advantageous to use a company in the first place.

TABLE 1

Self-Employed vs Corporation Tax 2017/18

Profits	Self Employed	Company	Saving
£10,000	£313	£1,900	-£1,587
£20,000	£2,913	£3,800	-£887
£30,000	£5,813	£5,700	£113
£40,000	£8,713	£7,600	£1,113
£50,000	£12,263	£9,500	£2,763
£60,000	£16,463	£11,400	£5,063
£70,000	£20,663	£13,300	£7,363
£80,000	£24,863	£15,200	£9,663
£90,000	£29,063	£17,100	£11,963
£100,000	£33,263	£19,000	£14,263

Table 1 compares the total income tax and national insurance paid by self-employed business owners with the corporation tax paid by companies. (Self-employed business owners in Scotland pay an additional £400 income tax if their profits exceed £45,000.)

Clearly companies don't always pay less tax than self-employed business owners, especially when profits are small. However, as profits increase so do the tax savings.

A business owner who uses a company will potentially have far more after-tax profit left to reinvest and grow the business. It is in these circumstances – when profits are reinvested – that companies are normally most powerful as tax shelters.

Profit Extraction = Additional Tax?

Table 1 may be misleading because it doesn't include the tax paid on any income extracted by the company owner.

Most company owners need to extract money for their own personal use. At this point an additional income tax and national insurance charge may arise.

The good news is that by carefully structuring your pay it is possible to minimise these additional tax charges. That's what this guide is all about!

However, it's worth making one final point. Following the recent increase in dividend tax rates, many company owners now pay more tax than self-employed business owners, sometimes *a lot* more tax.

For more information see the Taxcafe guide *Using a Company to Save Tax* which examines the pros and cons of being self employed with the pros and cons of using a company.

Chapter 2

How Directors Are Taxed: Employment Income

When HMRC and tax professionals talk about 'employment income', they are referring to salaries and bonuses.

Salaries and bonuses are subject to income tax and national insurance. They are also generally a tax deductible expense for the company.

Income Tax

For the 2017/18 tax year, starting on 6 April 2017, most individuals pay income tax as follows on their salaries:

- 0%   on the first   £11,500   Personal allowance
- 20% on the next   £33,500   Basic-rate band
- 40% above   £45,000   Higher-rate threshold

Generally speaking, if you earn more than £45,000 you are a higher-rate taxpayer; if you earn less you are a basic-rate taxpayer.

The number £45,000 is important to remember because it will be mentioned repeatedly in the chapters that follow.

Transferable Personal Allowance

It is now possible to transfer 10% of your personal allowance to your spouse or civil partner (£1,150 during the current 2017/18 tax year).

Only basic-rate taxpayers can benefit from this tax break, so the potential tax saving is £230 (£1,150 x 20%).

Unmarried couples are excluded – this was the rather feeble attempt by David Cameron (remember him?) to use the tax system to reward marriage.

Married couples can generally only benefit from this tax break if:

- One person earns less than £11,500 (not including savings interest under £5,000) and is therefore wasting some of their personal allowance

- The other person earns less than £45,000 (i.e. is a basic-rate taxpayer)

Both individuals must have been born on or after 6 April 1935.

You have to register to use it:

www.gov.uk/marriageallowance

Potential winners are married couples where one person does not work (e.g. full-time parents) or only has a part-time job.

Example
In 2017/18 Bill earns a salary of £30,000 and his wife Daphne earns £6,000 working part time. Daphne has £5,500 of unused personal allowance. She can transfer £1,150 of this to Bill which means Bill no longer has to pay tax on £1,150 of his income. This will save him £230 in tax (£1,150 x 20%).

Company owners have more scope than regular salaried employees to benefit from this tax giveaway, as we shall see in Chapter 20.

Income over £100,000

When your taxable income exceeds £100,000 your income tax personal allowance is gradually withdrawn. For every additional £1 you earn, 50p of your personal allowance is taken away.

What this means is that, when your income reaches £123,000, your personal allowance will have completely disappeared.

It also means that those who earn salary income between £100,000 and £123,000 face a marginal income tax rate of 60%.

Example

Caroline, a company director, has received salary income of £100,000 so far during the current tax year. If she receives an extra £100 of salary she will pay an extra £40 of income tax. She will also lose £50 of her income tax personal allowance, so £50 of previously tax-free salary will now be taxed at 40%, adding £20 to her tax bill.

All in all, she pays £60 in tax on her extra £100 of salary, so her marginal income tax rate is 60%.

Income above £150,000

Once your taxable income exceeds £150,000, you will pay 45% income tax on any extra employment income. This is known as the additional rate of tax. It used to be 50%.

National Insurance

For the current 2017/18 tax year individuals pay national insurance as follows on their salary income:

- 0% on the first £8,164 Primary threshold
- 12% on the next £36,836
- 2% above £45,000 Upper earnings limit

Combined Tax Rates

The combined marginal rates of income tax and national insurance applying to salaries in 2017/18 are as follows:

Income up to £8,164	0%
Income from £8,164 to £11,500	12%
Income from £11,500 to £45,000	32%
Income from £45,000 to £100,000	42%
Income from £100,000 to £123,000	62%
Income from £123,000 to £150,000	42%
Income over £150,000	47%

Employer's National Insurance

Most employees don't lose sleep over their employer's national insurance bill. However, as a company director/shareholder, the company's money is effectively your money so this extra tax is an important consideration.

Companies pay 13.8% national insurance on every single pound of salary the director/shareholder earns over the 'secondary threshold'. The secondary threshold is now the same as the primary threshold, i.e. £8,164 or £157 per week for 2017/18.

Employer's national insurance is, however, a tax deductible expense for corporation tax purposes. For example, if a company pays £100 of national insurance this will reduce its taxable profits by £100, saving the company at least £19 in corporation tax. So the net overall cost is £81.

There is no employer's national insurance on salaries paid to under 21s and apprentices under 25 provided, in both cases, they are not higher-rate taxpayers (i.e. they must earn less than £45,000).

£3,000 Employment Allowance

Most businesses qualify for the employment allowance, which provides a saving of up to £3,000 per year in employer's national insurance. It used to be £2,000 but was increased in April 2016.

The reason for covering the employment allowance in this guide is because it may affect some company owners' own salary choice.

For example, two company owners who have no other employees can pay themselves a salary of around £19,000 each this year without having to pay any employer's national insurance.

But is it a good idea to take this much salary to avoid wasting the £3,000 employment allowance? We'll answer this question in Chapter 7. In this section we'll take a brief look at some of the employment allowance rules.

One Man Band Companies

Unfortunately the employment allowance is no longer available to "one man band" companies where there is just one director who is the only employee.

According to HMRC guidance, the employment allowance also cannot be claimed if there are other employees BUT the director's salary is the only one on which employer's national insurance is payable.

This is to prevent directors of one-man band companies employing friends or family and paying them a token amount in order to claim the employment allowance for their own salaries.

At least one of the additional employees must be paid more than the secondary threshold. For example, a company that employs a seasonal worker who earns above the secondary threshold in a week (£157 for 2017/18) will be eligible for the employment allowance for the whole tax year.

The second employee can be another director (e.g. your spouse) provided both directors' salaries exceed the *annual* secondary threshold (£8,164 for 2017/18 or pro rata if the directorship begins after the tax year has started).

If circumstances change during the tax year and the director becomes the only employee paid above the secondary threshold, the employment allowance can still be claimed for that tax year.

If a company with just one director who earns less than the national insurance threshold employs just one other person (not a director), the company can claim the employment allowance if the employee earns more than the national insurance threshold.

It should be pointed out that several expert commentators, including the Institute of Chartered Accountants, believe HMRC has not interpreted the law correctly and that it should be possible to claim the employment allowance even if the second employee receives a token salary on which no employer's national insurance is payable. However, to be safe and avoid problems, it may nevertheless be necessary to pay a second employee a salary slightly higher than the secondary threshold.

Other Employment Allowance Rules

The employment allowance can only be used against class 1 national insurance and not against class 1A national insurance. Class 1A is due on most taxable benefits provided to employees, e.g. company cars.

If your company belongs to a group of companies, only one can claim the allowance. If your business runs multiple PAYE schemes, the allowance can only be claimed against one scheme.

The allowance is claimed as part of the payroll process. The full £3,000 can be claimed in month one of the tax year if your employer's class 1 national insurance exceeds £3,000 per month.

You can start claiming the allowance after the tax year has started and make a catch-up claim which can also be offset against your other PAYE costs.

If you claim the allowance at the end of the tax year and your remaining PAYE costs are not sufficient to use the entire allowance, the unclaimed balance can be carried forward to the next tax year.

Connected Companies

A company cannot claim the employment allowance if a 'connected company' already claims it. Companies are connected if one company has control of the other company or both companies are controlled by the same person.

A person is generally considered to have control of a company if they hold more than 50% of the company's share capital or voting power or if they are entitled to more than 50% of the company's distributable income or assets if the company is wound up.

For example, if you own all the shares in two companies you will only be entitled to one employment allowance, even if the two companies are completely separate businesses with, for example, separate premises and staff.

If the company that claims the employment allowance has employer's class 1 national insurance of less than £3,000, the balance cannot be claimed by the other company.

Where there is 'substantial commercial interdependence' between two or more companies the holdings of close relatives and other 'associates' are added together to determine whether they are controlled by the same person or group of persons.

For example, if you own all the shares in company X and your spouse owns all the shares in company Y, your spouse's holding in company Y is attributed to you and you are treated as controlling company X and Y, as is your spouse. However, the two companies will only be treated as connected companies if there is substantial commercial interdependence between them.

If the two companies are completely unrelated then two employment allowances can be claimed. If there is substantial commercial interdependence between the companies then only one allowance can be claimed.

The definition of associates is broad but would typically include spouses, parents and grandparents, children and grandchildren, brothers and sisters, business partners and certain trusts.

To determine whether there is substantial commercial interdependence between two companies one or more of the following must be present:

- **Financial interdependence** – Two companies are financially interdependent if one gives financial support to the other or each has a financial interest in the same business.

- **Economic interdependence** – Two companies are economically interdependent if they have the same economic objective or the activities of one benefits the other or they have common customers.

- **Organisational interdependence** – Two companies are organisationally interdependent if they have common management, employees, premises or equipment.

Case Study – Total Tax Payable on Salary

Jane earns a salary of £60,000. Her income tax for 2017/18 can be calculated as follows:

- 0% on the first £11,500 = £0
- 20% on the next £33,500 = £6,700
- 40% on the final £15,000 = £6,000

Total income tax bill: £12,700

Her national insurance for 2017/18 can be calculated as follows:

- 0% on the first £8,164 = £0
- 12% on the next £36,836 = £4,420
- 2% on the final £15,000 = £300

Jane's national insurance bill: £4,720.

Her company claims the £3,000 employment allowance but this is used up paying salaries to other employees. Her company's national insurance bill on her salary is therefore:

- 0%   on the first £8,164 = £0
- 13.8% on the next £51,836 = £7,153

The company's national insurance bill is £7,153. Because the company pays corporation tax at 19%, its national insurance bill, net of corporation tax relief, is £5,794.

The total tax paid by Jane and her company is as follows:

	£
Income tax	£12,700
Employee's national insurance	£4,720
Employer's national insurance	£5,794
Total taxes	£23,214

When you include employer's national insurance, it's startling how much tax is paid on Jane's income. Her £60,000 salary is not low by any standards but you wouldn't describe her as a high income earner either. Nevertheless an amount equivalent to 39% of her salary is paid in direct taxes on her *whole* income.

TABLE 2
Total Tax Payable on Salary 2017/18

Salary	Income Tax	Employee NI	Employer NI	Total	%
10,000	0	220	205	426	4
20,000	1,700	1,420	1,323	4,443	22
30,000	3,700	2,620	2,441	8,761	29
40,000	5,700	3,820	3,559	13,079	33
50,000	8,700	4,520	4,676	17,897	36
60,000	12,700	4,720	5,794	23,214	39
70,000	16,700	4,920	6,912	28,532	41
80,000	20,700	5,120	8,030	33,850	42
90,000	24,700	5,320	9,148	39,168	44
100,000	28,700	5,520	10,265	44,486	44
110,000	34,700	5,720	11,383	51,804	47
120,000	40,700	5,920	12,501	59,121	49
130,000	45,300	6,120	13,619	65,039	50
140,000	49,300	6,320	14,737	70,357	50
150,000	53,300	6,520	15,854	75,675	50
160,000	57,800	6,720	16,972	81,493	51
170,000	62,300	6,920	18,090	87,310	51
180,000	66,800	7,120	19,208	93,128	52
190,000	71,300	7,320	20,326	98,946	52
200,000	75,800	7,520	21,443	104,764	52
225,000	87,050	8,020	24,238	119,308	53
250,000	98,300	8,520	27,032	133,853	54
275,000	109,550	9,020	29,827	148,397	54
300,000	120,800	9,520	32,621	162,942	54
350,000	143,300	10,520	38,210	192,031	55
400,000	165,800	11,520	43,799	221,120	55
450,000	188,300	12,520	49,388	250,209	56
500,000	210,800	13,520	54,977	279,298	56
600,000	255,800	15,520	66,155	337,476	56
700,000	300,800	17,520	77,333	395,654	57
800,000	345,800	19,520	88,511	453,832	57
900,000	390,800	21,520	99,689	512,010	57
1,000,000	435,800	23,520	110,867	570,188	57

Table 2 shows the total tax payable on a whole range of salaries. In each case we assume the director's salary is subject to employer's national insurance which is not reduced by the £3,000 employment allowance. The employer's national insurance cost has been reduced by deducting 19% corporation tax relief.

Once again, it's startling how much tax is paid on salaries, especially when you look at the overall tax rate (the last column in the table).

Future Income Tax Changes

Income Tax Rates and Thresholds

In their 2017 election manifesto the Conservatives committed once again to raising the personal allowance to £12,500 by 2020 and the higher-rate threshold to £50,000.

The Tax Lock

Legislation was passed to keep income tax rates fixed until 2020/21, as well as the national insurance rates paid by employers and employees. VAT increases were also barred by this legislation.

The 2017 Conservative election manifesto does not contain the same commitments, except a promise to not increase VAT. Instead it contains the following rather wishy-washy assurance:

"The Conservatives will always be the party that keeps tax as low as possible and spends the proceeds responsibly. It is our firm intention to reduce taxes on Britain's businesses and working families."

Scottish Tax

The Scottish Parliament now has complete power to set income tax rates and thresholds.

This means it can, for example, put up the 45% additional rate of tax without increasing the basic rate or higher rate and change the thresholds where the various tax rates kick in. It can also create entirely new income tax bands and rates.

The Scottish Parliament has the power to tax salaries, self-employment income, rental income and pensions.

It does NOT have the power to tax savings (interest) and dividend income. Dividends, including small company dividends, continue to be taxed using UK rates and thresholds.

The Scottish Parliament also does not have the power to set the personal allowance, although in practice it can increase it by introducing a new 0% tax bracket.

National insurance and most other taxes, including corporation tax, capital gains tax and inheritance tax, remain the preserve of the UK Government.

Scottish Income Tax 2017/18

In 2017/18 Scottish income tax is the same as the rest of the UK with one important exception: the higher-rate threshold is frozen at £43,000 (the threshold is £45,000 in the rest of the UK). As a result, Scots pay income tax as follows on most types of income:

- 0% on the first   £11,500
- 20% on the next   £31,500
- 40% above   £43,000

Scots who earn over £45,000 will pay £400 more tax than those who live in the rest of the UK. This "tartan tax gap" is likely to increase over the next few years as the UK Government raises the higher-rate threshold to £50,000.

Thus the tax bills listed in Table 2 must all be increased by £400 if you live in Scotland and earn more than £45,000.

Who is a Scottish Taxpayer?

Someone is a Scottish taxpayer if their sole or main place of residence is in Scotland.

For example, someone who rents a flat in London where they work during the week will probably be treated as a Scottish taxpayer if their spouse and children live in the family home in

Edinburgh and most of their friends and other social links are also in Edinburgh.

In some cases it may be difficult to establish where the main residence is located.

Where no close connection to Scotland can be identified (for example, because it is not possible to establish the person's main place of residence), Scottish taxpayer status will be determined through day counting.

You will be a Scottish taxpayer if you spend more days during the tax year in Scotland than you spend in Wales, Northern Ireland or England (taking each country separately).

Scottish Company Owners

If a Scottish company owner pays himself a small tax-free salary (see Chapter 7) and takes the rest of his income as dividends he will not be affected by Scottish income tax and will pay the same amount of tax as company owners in the rest of the UK.

This is because the Scottish Parliament cannot change the income tax personal allowance or the national insurance thresholds and cannot tax dividend income.

(Up until recently I would have said that this is a blessing... but that was before the UK Government, and a *Conservative* one at that, decided to increase the tax rates for dividend income!)

If a Scottish company owner has salary and rental income of more than £43,000 this year he will start paying 40% tax and will pay up to £400 more tax than someone with the same income living in another part of the UK.

Chapter 3

How Directors Are Taxed: Dividend Income

Dividends are subject to income tax but not national insurance. Also, the income tax rates on dividends are lower than the income tax rates on salaries because dividends are paid out of a company's *after-tax* profits: the money has already been taxed in the company's hands, whereas salaries are a tax deductible expense.

The tax treatment of dividends has been completely changed with effect from 6 April 2016.

Dividend tax credits have been abolished, so it is no longer necessary to gross up your cash dividends to calculate your tax. All tax calculations now work with cash dividends only and are therefore a lot simpler.

(I generally refer to the amount of dividend actually paid, or deemed to be paid, as the "cash" dividend. This does not necessarily mean that it is literally paid in cash, as dividends are sometimes paid by way of accounting entries.)

While simpler tax calculations are the good news, the bad news is that new tax rates for cash dividends have been introduced that are 7.5% higher than the previous ones.

The first £5,000 of dividend income you receive is, however, tax free thanks to the "dividend nil rate band", also known as the "dividend allowance". Unfortunately, the dividend allowance will be cut to £2,000 in 2018/19.

For those receiving dividends in excess of the £5,000 dividend allowance, the following income tax rates now apply (the old effective rates are included for comparison):

	Old	**Current**
Basic-rate taxpayers	0%	7.5%
Higher-rate taxpayers	25%	32.5%
Additional-rate taxpayers	30.6%	38.1%

Overall Tax Rates on Dividend Income

Because income paid out as dividends is taxed twice (first in the hands of the company and second in the hands of the shareholder) it's easy to lose sight of how much tax is being paid overall.

As a company owner you are likely to be equally concerned about your company's tax bill as your own, so it's worth showing the overall combined tax rate on dividend income.

With companies now paying 19% corporation tax, the total tax rates on dividend income are as follows:

	Total Tax Rate (rounded)
Basic-rate taxpayers	25%
Higher-rate taxpayers	45%
Additional-rate taxpayers	50%

For example, a company with £100 of profit will pay £19 corporation tax, leaving £81 to pay out as dividends. Ignoring the £5,000 dividend allowance, a higher-rate taxpayer will pay £26 tax on this income (£81 x 32.5%), so the total tax bill on the £100 profit is £45, which is 45%.

The above tax rates are higher than the regular income tax rates that apply to most types of income (20% for basic-rate taxpayers, 40% for higher-rate taxpayers and 45% for additional-rate taxpayers).

This is because the Government wants to level the playing field between company owners (who often don't pay any national insurance) and self-employed business owners and regular employees, who pay national insurance on most of their earnings.

From a tax planning perspective, once they've used up the £5,000 dividend allowance, company owners may now be better off paying themselves income that is taxed at "regular" income tax rates in preference to dividends, wherever possible.

An obvious example would be rental income. A small salary also fits the bill, as we shall see shortly, as long as the additional national insurance cost is mitigated.

Cash Dividends = Lower Taxable Income

Dividend tax rates have gone up but the thresholds where they kick in have gone up too. This is because dividends are no longer grossed up, artificially pushing you into a higher tax bracket.

In other words, you can now extract more dividend income from your company before you become a higher-rate taxpayer and before you lose your child benefit or personal allowance or become an additional-rate taxpayer. For example, under the old system of grossing up dividends a company owner with no other income would have been able to withdraw a cash dividend of £40,500 this year (£45,000 x 0.9) before becoming a higher-rate taxpayer. Under the current system you can take a cash dividend of £45,000 before becoming a higher-rate taxpayer and paying 32.5% tax.

Don't be mistaken, almost every company owner pays more tax under the new regime but for some the pain is reduced by having more income falling into a lower tax bracket.

The £5,000 Dividend Nil Rate Band

Company owners do not enjoy an additional standalone amount of £5,000 tax free. Instead, the dividend nil rate band typically uses up some of your basic-rate band.

If you have a £50,000 dividend and no other income, the first £11,500 will be tax free thanks to your personal allowance and the next £5,000 will be tax free thanks to the dividend nil rate band. Only £28,500 of your remaining income will be taxed at 7.5% because the £5,000 dividend nil rate band uses up part of your £33,500 basic-rate band. The final £5,000 will be taxed at 32.5%.

The dividend nil rate band only uses up your basic-rate band if, like many company owners, you have dividend income subject to basic-rate tax. As we shall see later, it works differently if you have a lot of other income and all your dividends are subject to higher-rate tax.

Note the reduction in the dividend allowance to £2,000 in April 2018 was dropped from the 2017 Finance Act because of the general election. It is understood the Government will legislate for this and other dropped measures at the earliest opportunity.

The New Dividend Tax Regime – Examples

Let's take a look at some sample dividend tax calculations. To keep things simple we'll assume that the company owners take a small salary of £8,164 and the rest of their income as dividends (see Chapter 7 for why this is often tax-efficient). We'll also assume in each case that the company owners have no other taxable income. All of the examples apply equally to Scottish company owners.

Example – Basic-Rate Taxpayer

Stuart is a company owner with a salary of £8,164 and cash dividend of £20,000. His total income is thus £28,164.

His salary is tax-free because it is covered by his personal allowance. The first £3,336 of his dividend income is tax free, being covered by the remainder of his personal allowance (£11,500 - £8,164).

The next £5,000 of his dividend income is also tax-free thanks to the dividend allowance. The final £11,664 of his dividend income is taxed at 7.5%, producing a total tax bill of £875.

As an aside, Stuart's tax bill would have been £0 under the old dividend tax regime.

Example – Higher-Rate Taxpayer

Robert is a company owner with a salary of £8,164 and dividend of £37,000. His total income is thus £45,164.

His salary is tax-free as it is covered by his personal allowance, as is the first £3,336 of his dividend (£11,500 -£8,164).

The next £5,000 of his dividend is also tax-free thanks to the dividend allowance. The dividend allowance uses up £5,000 of his £33,500 basic-rate band so just £28,500 of his dividend income is taxed at 7.5%, producing a tax bill of £2,138. The final £164 of his dividend income takes him over the higher-rate threshold and is taxed at 32.5%, producing a tax bill of £53.

Robert's total tax bill is £2,191 in 2017/18 (he would have paid £962 tax under the old dividend tax regime).

Example – Personal Allowance Withdrawal

Alpesh is a company owner with a salary of £8,164 and dividend of £100,000. His total taxable income is thus £108,164. His personal allowance is reduced from £11,500 to £7,418. Thus £746 of his salary is taxed at 20% (£8,164 - £7,418), producing a tax bill of £149.

The first £5,000 of his dividend income is tax free, being covered by the dividend allowance. The next £27,754 of his dividend income is covered by his remaining basic-rate band (£33,500 - £746 - £5,000) and taxed at 7.5%, producing a tax bill of £2,082.

The remaining £67,246 of his dividend income is taxed at 32.5%, producing a tax bill of £21,855.

His total tax bill is therefore £24,086 (he would have paid £20,140 tax under the old dividend tax regime).

Example – Additional-Rate Taxpayer

Maeve is a company owner with a salary of £8,164 and dividend of £200,000. Her total income is thus £208,164. Because her income exceeds £150,000 she is an additional-rate taxpayer.

The first £5,000 of her dividend income is tax free but her income tax personal allowance is completely withdrawn. This means she will pay 20% income tax on her salary – £1,633 – and her remaining basic-rate band will be reduced to just £20,336 (£33,500 - £8,164 salary - £5,000 dividend allowance). She will thus pay 7.5% tax on £20,336 of her dividend income (£1,525).

The next £116,500 of her dividend (£150,000 less £33,500) is subject to higher-rate tax at 32.5%, resulting in additional tax of £37,863. The remaining £58,164 of dividend income takes her over the £150,000 threshold and is taxed at 38.1%, resulting in additional tax of £22,160.

Maeve's total tax bill is £63,181 (she would have paid £49,952 under the old dividend tax regime).

Taxpayers with Lots of Non-Dividend Income

It's important to explain how the new dividend nil rate band operates when you have lots of non-dividend income, for example a big salary or a significant amount of rental income.

The dividend nil rate band only forms part of your basic-rate band if you have dividend income that falls into the basic-rate band. It works differently if your basic-rate band is completely used up by other income, e.g. salary or rental income.

The way to think about it is like this: dividends are always treated as the top slice of your income and taxed at your highest marginal rate. The dividend nil rate band exempts the bottom £5,000 of that income from tax. So if you have dividend income taxed at both 7.5% and 32.5%, the dividend allowance will exempt some of the income taxed at 7.5%.

But if ALL of your dividend income is taxed at 32.5% (because you have lots of other income, e.g. rental income) the dividend nil rate band will be part of your higher-rate band and you'll pay 0% tax instead of 32.5% tax on £5,000 of your dividend income.

Example
In 2017/18 Brendan has a £42,000 salary and £10,000 dividend. The first £11,500 of his salary is covered by his personal allowance and the next £30,500 falls into the basic-rate band where it's taxed at 20%; leaving him with £3,000 of basic-rate band available. £5,000 of his dividend income is tax free, thanks to the dividend allowance. The first £3,000 uses up the remainder of his basic-rate band, leaving £2,000 of dividend allowance to use in the higher-rate band. The remaining £5,000 of his dividend income is taxed at the 32.5% higher rate.

Example
In 2017/18 Julia has a £45,000 salary and £30,000 dividend. Her salary uses up her personal allowance and basic-rate band, taking her to the higher-rate threshold. The first £5,000 of her dividend is covered by the dividend allowance; £25,000 is taxed at the 32.5% higher rate.

The dividend allowance does not form part of her basic-rate band because none of her dividend income falls into the basic-rate band.

Example

In 2017/18 Leon has a £130,000 salary and £50,000 dividend. With this much income his personal allowance is completely withdrawn.

The first £5,000 of his dividend income is covered by the dividend allowance, leaving £15,000 taxed at the 32.5% higher rate. Along with his salary this takes Leon up to the £150,000 additional-rate threshold. The final £30,000 of his dividend income is taxed at 38.1%.

Note, Leon has dividend income taxed at both the higher rate and additional rate. The dividend allowance reduces the amount of his dividend income taxed at the 32.5% higher rate.

Example

In 2017/18 Martin has a £100,000 salary, £50,000 of rental income and £50,000 dividend. With this much income his personal allowance is completely withdrawn.

His salary and rental income take him up to the £150,000 additional-rate threshold. The first £5,000 of his dividend income is covered by the dividend allowance, leaving £45,000 taxed at the 38.1% additional rate.

All of Martin's dividend income is taxable at the additional rate. The dividend allowance therefore reduces the amount of his dividend income taxed at the additional rate.

Scottish Taxpayers

The Scottish Parliament can set the income tax rates and thresholds for most types of income BUT not dividends or interest.

For the current 2017/18 tax year the only difference between Scotland and the rest of the UK is the higher-rate threshold, which is £43,000 in Scotland and £45,000 in the rest of the UK.

The £45,000 threshold applies to dividend and interest income.

Interest income is covered further in chapters 19 and 24. The practical implications for Scottish company owners with dividend income are the following:

- **Other income £43,000 or less**. If your other income (e.g. salary and rental income) is less than £43,000 you will pay exactly the same amount of tax on ALL your income as taxpayers in the rest of the UK. You'll only pay 32.5% tax on your dividends once your income rises above £45,000. Additional tax: None.

- **Other income between £43,000 and £45,000**. For example, if your salary and rental income is £44,000 you will pay an additional £200 tax on £1,000 of that income. The first £1,000 of your dividend income will be tax free thanks to the dividend allowance, taking you up to the £45,000 higher-rate threshold. The next £4,000 of your dividends will also be tax free; after that you'll start paying 32.5% tax. Additional tax £200.

- **Other income £45,000 or more**. If your other income (e.g. salary and rental income) is more than £45,000 you will pay 32.5% on your dividends, just like taxpayers in the rest of the UK (although the first £5,000 will be tax free). The only difference is you will pay an extra £400 tax on your other income. Additional tax: £400.

Looking at the last set of examples, if Julia, Leon and Martin lived in Scotland they would all pay an additional £400 in tax (because their salaries and other non-dividend income are £45,000 or more). However, Brendan's tax bill will be the same, whether he lives in Scotland or another part of the UK.

Will Dividend Tax Rates be Increased Again?

When the dividend tax increase was announced in the July 2015 Budget the documentation stated that:

"These changes will also start to reduce the incentive to incorporate and remunerate through dividends rather than through wages to reduce tax liabilities."

Use of the word "start" hinted that further dividend tax increases were on the horizon. In the March 2017 Budget the threat became reality when it was announced that the dividend allowance will be reduced from £5,000 to £2,000 in April 2018.

The Government has a bee in its bonnet about the different amounts of tax paid by salaried employees, the self-employed (sole traders and partnerships) and company owners. It's quite clear that those in charge of tax policy do not believe that entrepreneurs should be given special tax treatment to foster economic growth.

This is why the rate of class 4 national insurance paid by the self-employed was increased in the March 2017 Budget and the dividend allowance was cut. The national insurance increase was later canned when the media pointed out that it broke the 2015 election pledge to not increase tax rates... but none of the recent dividend tax increases were reversed.

So it would appear that tax policy is as haphazard as ever and company owners can expect little sympathy from the press or the Government. For this reason, we would not rule out further tax increases in the future.

Dividend Tax Terminology

Note that the 0% tax rate applying to the £5,000 dividend nil rate band is known officially as the "dividend nil rate". The 7.5% rate is known as the "ordinary rate", the 32.5% rate is known as the "upper rate" and the 38.1% rate as the "additional rate".

I do not use these terms much in this guide, preferring the terms basic rate, higher rate and additional rate.

Chapter 4

Don't Forget about Payments on Account

With the increase in dividend tax rates many company owners face having to make payments on account for the first time.

Payments on account are made twice a year and allow HMRC to collect some of the tax you owe early. Common victims include sole traders and landlords, i.e. those whose income tax is not collected at source. Most salary earners do not have to make payments on account because their tax is collected almost immediately through PAYE.

Up until recently the only small company owners who had to make payments on account were higher-rate taxpayers. Basic-rate taxpayers didn't pay any tax on their dividends and therefore didn't have to make any payments on account.

This has all changed. Basic-rate taxpayers now have to pay 7.5% tax on their dividends and so many will now have to make twice yearly payments on account.

Note, payments on account are not extra tax but they do affect your cashflow.

How Payments on Account Are Calculated

If you paid yourself a dividend during the previous tax year, which started on 6 April 2016 and ended on 5 April 2017, the income tax is normally payable by 31 January 2018 – almost 10 months after the tax year has ended.

For example, let's say a company owner paid himself a salary of £11,000 and dividend of £25,000 and had no other taxable income. Let's also assume that he has not had to make any payments on account to date.

No income tax was payable on his salary because it was fully covered by his personal allowance and the first £5,000 of his dividend income is also be tax free thanks to the dividend nil rate band.

The remaining £20,000 of his dividend income is taxed at 7.5%, producing a total income tax bill of £1,500 which has to be paid by 31 January 2018.

2017/18 Tax Year

Now let's move forward to the 2017/18 tax year which started on 6 April 2017 and ends on 5 April 2018.

We will assume our company owner pays himself a tax-free salary of £11,500 and the same dividend of £25,000. His income tax bill will again be £1,500 but this time he cannot wait until 31 January 2019 to pay his tax.

On 31 January 2018, when he pays his 2016/17 tax bill, he will also have to make a £750 payment on account for 2017/18 and another one on 31 July 2018. Thus his total tax payments will be as follows:

- 31 January 2018   £1,500 + £750 = £2,250
- 31 July 2018   £750

Each payment on account is half the previous year's (2016/17) self assessment tax.

In January 2019 he will make his final tax payment for 2017/18 but will be able to deduct the two payments on account. In this example he will have no additional tax to pay because his payments on account will fully cover his tax bill.

But if he takes a bigger dividend in 2017/18 he will have to make a final balancing payment in January 2019 (because his payments on account will have been too small). And if he takes a smaller dividend in 2017/18 he will be entitled to a tax refund (because his payments on account will have been too big).

Postponing Tax

Making payments on account is still much better than paying tax through the PAYE system.

Take a look at our company owner's tax payments for 2017/18.

The first payment is due around *10 months* after the start of the tax year (January 2018) and the second payment is due around *16 months* after the start of the tax year (July 2018).

This means that if you pay yourself a dividend at the start of the tax year, you will have free use of the taxman's money for around 13 months on average.

That money could be invested in a cash ISA or an offset mortgage or some other low-risk investment. The returns are likely to be better than those available from your company's bank account.

Who Has to Make Payments on Account?

Payments on account are all about the tax you paid in the *previous tax year*.

You only have to make payments on account if your self-assessment tax (i.e. ignoring tax deducted at source) for the previous tax year was more than £1,000.

For example, if during the current 2017/18 tax year you pay yourself a salary of £11,500 and a dividend of £18,000 your total income tax bill will be £975 and you will not have to make any payments on account in January and July 2019.

Of course, if you have income from other sources (e.g. rental income from property) this will have to be factored into the equation too.

You do not have to make payments on account, however, if more than 80% of your total tax from the previous year was covered by tax deducted at source.

No payments on account are due in respect of capital gains tax.

How to Reduce Payments on Account

Where your self-assessment liability for the current year can reasonably be expected to be less than that for the previous year, you can apply to reduce your payments on account to the appropriate level (i.e. half of the anticipated liability for the current year).

For example, if you take a smaller dividend in 2017/18 than you took in 2016/17, you can apply to reduce your payments on account due on 31 January and 31 July 2018.

You can do this when you submit your 2016/17 tax return.

You have to be careful when doing this, however. If you claim a reduction in your payments on account and then find that you have more tax to pay than you expected, you will have to pay interest on the underpayment and potentially a penalty.

Chapter 5

Salary versus Dividends: The Basics

Unlike self-employed business owners (sole traders and partnerships), company owners are in the fortunate position of wearing two caps.

On the one hand, you can reward your work as a director; on the other hand, you can reward your entrepreneurship as a shareholder.

As a company director and shareholder you can split your income into salary and dividends and this can generate income tax and national insurance savings.

For example, while national insurance is payable on salaries, it is not payable on shareholder dividends.

By structuring distributions from your company carefully and taking the 'optimum' amount of salary and dividends, you could end up with a significantly higher after-tax income than a regular salaried employee who earns a higher income before tax.

However, while saving income tax will be an important consideration, other factors are important too.

Salaries & Dividends: What's the Difference?

The major differences between a salary and dividend are the following:

Salaries Are Tax Deductible

Salaries usually qualify for corporation tax relief, dividends do not.

If the company pays you a salary, its taxable profits will be reduced and it will pay less corporation tax.

Dividends are paid out of a company's after-tax profits, so paying a dividend does not reduce the *company's* tax bill.

This is an important point to remember because most company owners are concerned about both their own and their company's tax bill.

For example, if a company has a taxable profit of £10,000 it will pay £1900 in corporation tax (19%), leaving £8,100 available to distribute as dividends.

This corporation tax must be added to any income tax paid by the shareholder on his dividend income when calculating the total tax suffered.

Dividends Require Profits

Only companies that have made profits can pay dividends. Profits are usually calculated when the company's annual accounts are drawn up (often many months after the end of the company's financial year).

So dividends will usually be paid out of profits made in a previous accounting period. It is, however, possible to pay dividends out of profits made during the current year, for example if accurate management accounts are drawn up to determine the level of the company's distributable profits (see Chapter 34).

Salaries can be paid even if the company is making tax losses.

National Insurance

Salaries are generally subject to national insurance, dividends are not. Both the director and the company may be subject to national insurance.

Income Tax

Salaries and dividends are subject to different rates of income tax.

Tax Payment Dates

The income tax and national insurance payable on salaries is collected almost immediately via PAYE. The income tax on dividends is collected via self assessment – generally at a later date.

Earnings

Salaries are classed as 'earnings' which is important if you want to make significant pension contributions personally. Dividends are not classed as earnings.

Chapter 6

Company Owners Can Control Their Income Tax Bills

In Chapter 5 we mentioned that a company owner can often decide whether any distribution of the company's money is classified as salary or dividend.

Another advantage of being a company owner is that you have complete control over *how much* income you withdraw in total.

This gives you significant control over your personal income tax bill.

Unlike sole traders, who pay tax each year on ALL the profits of the business, company owners only pay income tax on the money they actually withdraw from the company.

This allows company owners to reduce their income tax bills by adopting the following strategies:

- 'Smooth income'
- 'Roller-coaster income'

Smooth Income

With smooth income, the company owner withdraws roughly the same amount of money each year, even though the company's profits may fluctuate considerably.

'Smooth income' allows the director/shareholder to stay below any of the following key income tax thresholds that could result in a higher income tax bill:

- £45,000   Higher-rate tax
- £50,000   Child benefit tax charge
- £100,000   Personal allowance withdrawal
- £150,000   Additional rate tax

We will return to how you can plan your salary and dividend withdrawals around these key income tax thresholds in the chapters that follow.

The last three thresholds didn't even exist a few years ago, which goes to show how much more complicated and burdensome the UK's income tax system has become for those considered to be 'high earners'.

Roller-coaster Income

With 'roller-coaster income', the directors/shareholders take a bigger or smaller salary or dividend than would normally be required to fund their lifestyles.

Roller-coaster income could save you tax in the following circumstances:

Tax Rates Are Going Up Or Down

If the Government announces that tax rates will *rise* during a future tax year, you may wish to pay yourself more income now and less income later on.

And if your tax rate will *fall* during a future tax year, you should pay yourself less income now and more income later on.

You Want to Avoid Capital Gains Tax

It may also make sense for company owners to pay themselves less income during tax years in which they sell assets subject to capital gains tax, e.g. rental properties.

Why? This may allow some of your basic-rate band (£33,500 in 2017/18) to be freed up, which means some of your capital gains will be taxed at 10% or 18% instead of 20% or 28% (see Chapter 38).

Living Abroad

If you intend to move abroad and become non-resident in the future, you could consider withdrawing less income from your company while you are UK resident and more income after you become non-resident.

Providing you move to a country with favourable income tax rates, this strategy could potentially save you significant amounts of UK income tax (but see Chapter 39 for potential dangers).

Pension Income

When you reach age 55 you may decide to start withdrawing money from any private pension scheme you belong to, for example a self-invested personal pension (SIPP). Any amount you withdraw over and above your 25% tax-free lump sum will be subject to income tax.

Fortunately, with a drawdown arrangement you can vary the amount of income you withdraw from your pension scheme every year and there are no limits placed on the amount of income you can withdraw.

Coupled with the fact that you can vary the amount of income you withdraw from your company, this could allow you to minimise your income tax bill by staying below any of the income tax thresholds listed earlier.

Part 2

Tax-free Salaries & Dividends

Chapter 7

Tax-free Salaries

After reading the preceding chapters you should have a good understanding of how salaries and dividends are taxed.

The next question is: What is the most tax-efficient mix of salary and dividends for directors/shareholders who want to extract money from their companies?

In this chapter we will attempt to calculate the "optimal" amount of salary you should withdraw from your company.

The answer depends on various factors including whether your company's £3,000 national insurance employment allowance is used up paying salaries to other employees.

All amounts are for the current tax year which ends on 5 April 2018. The answer changes every year, so make sure you stay up to date.

Assumption: No Other Taxable Income

We will assume for now that the director/shareholder has no other taxable income. This keeps the number crunching as simple as possible.

It's not a totally unrealistic assumption either. Although most company directors have at least some other taxable income, for example some bank account interest or stock market dividends, many have no more than a few hundred pounds.

For those director/shareholders who do have significant amounts of other taxable income, for example rental profits from a portfolio of properties, more information is provided in Part 4.

Why a Small Salary Is Tax Efficient

The first point to make is that most company owners should not pay themselves just dividends and no salary.

The first few thousand pounds of either salary or dividends are tax-free in the hands of the director/shareholder, if the payments fall within the various income tax and national insurance thresholds.

However, a dividend payment is not necessarily tax efficient for the *company* (and, of course, most company owners are equally concerned about their company's tax position as their own personal tax position).

Dividends are paid out of a company's *after-tax* profits, i.e., after corporation tax has been paid. So every dividend has a corporation tax bill attached to it.

A salary, on the other hand, is a tax deductible expense for the company. Salaries are subject to national insurance (both for the director and the company) but salaries below £8,164 have no national insurance consequences.

In summary, a small salary is much more tax efficient than a dividend. Not only is it tax free in the hands of the director/shareholder, it provides a corporation tax saving for the company as well.

This corporation tax saving is essentially a cashback for the company and is why the director/shareholder should consider paying a salary, even if the money isn't needed.

For the same reason, the director/shareholder should consider paying salaries to their spouse or partner and children, including their minor children wherever possible (see Part 5).

How Much Salary?
Companies with Employees
(i.e. with no spare employment allowance)

We'll start off with owners of companies whose £3,000 employment allowance (see Chapter 2) is already used up paying salaries to other employees, i.e. there is no spare employment allowance for the directors own salaries.

This section also applies to "one man band" companies with just one director who is the only employee and other companies that aren't entitled to the employment allowance (see Chapter 2).

So how much salary should a company owner in this situation take? There are two important thresholds for the 2017/18 tax year:

- National insurance   £8,164
- Income tax   £11,500

For 2017/18 the "optimal" salary for many directors of companies with no spare employment allowance is £8,164.

A salary of £8,164 will not attract any employee or employer national insurance and, providing the director/shareholder has no other income, will also be free from income tax.

Before the 2017/18 tax year there were two different national insurance thresholds: one for employees and one for employers. However, these have now been permanently aligned and will be increased each year in line with CPI inflation.

Because salaries are usually a tax deductible expense, a salary of £8,164 will also save the company £1,551 in corporation tax:

£8,164 x 19% corporation tax = £1,551

In other words, it will cost the company just £6,613 to put £8,164 of tax-free cash in the hands of the director/shareholder.

I placed the word "optimal" in inverted commas because every company and owner is different. Clearly, a salary of £8,164 will not be optimal for every single company owner in the land. There are many other factors that may influence your salary decision.

Salary of £11,500?

Why not take a salary of £11,500 instead of £8,164 to use up your income tax personal allowance? Because the extra salary will attract both employee's and employer's national insurance, at 12% and 13.8% respectively:

Extra national insurance cost

Employee's NI   £11,500 - £8,164 = £3,336 x 12%   = £400
Employer's NI   £11,500 - £8,164 = £3,336 x 13.8% = £460

On the plus side, the extra salary and employer's national insurance will attract corporation tax relief at 19%:

Extra corporation tax relief

£3,336 x 19% = £634
£460   x 19% = £87

The extra national insurance cost (£860) outweighs the extra corporation tax relief (£721) by £139.

Extra tax on dividends

That's not the end of the story. Where the directors withdraw the company's remaining profits as dividends the higher salary will use up the final £3,336 of their personal allowances, which means £3,336 of dividend income which would have been tax free will now typically be taxed at 7.5% or 32.5%.

On the plus side, the additional salary and employer's national insurance will reduce the amount of after-tax profit available to distribute as dividends by £3,075 (£3,336 + £460 less 19% corporation tax), which will reduce the amount of dividend income on which the directors pay tax.

The net effect of all this is that basic-rate taxpayers will typically be around £160 worse off by taking a salary of £11,500 instead of £8,164 and many higher-rate taxpayers will typically be around £225 worse off.

Summary

Clearly the extra tax cost is not significant, so whether you take a salary of £8,164, £11,500 or something in between, probably won't make a huge amount of difference to many company directors at the end of the day.

Some company owners may wish to pay themselves a salary of £11,500 because, although strictly speaking not "optimal", this lets them take a bigger chunk of income out of the company on a regular basis, without some of the hassle that comes with paying dividends (for example, making sure the company has sufficient distributable profits and that dividends are properly declared).

Although the tax savings are fairly trivial, this juggling act gets to the heart of the salary/dividend question: as a company owner you have to compare the tax cost to you *personally* with the tax cost and tax relief enjoyed by your *company*.

In summary, for the remainder of this guide we will assume that directors whose companies have no spare employment allowance (e.g. where it's used up paying salaries to other employees) take a salary of £8,164 during the 2017/18 tax year, although a salary of up to £11,500 can be taken with very little additional tax cost.

How Much Salary?
Companies with No Employees
(i.e. with spare employment allowance)

In this section we'll take a look at companies that do NOT use up their £3,000 employment allowance paying salaries to other employees, i.e. there is spare employment allowance for the directors own salaries.

This group includes companies with no employees other than the directors and companies with just a couple of low-paid employees (please see Chapter 2 for more information about which companies qualify for the employment allowance).

Directors of these companies may be able to pay themselves higher salaries without having to worry about *employer's* national insurance. The question is, should they?

Salary of £11,500?

If the company owner takes a salary of £11,500 instead of £8,164 no national insurance will be paid by the company itself but the extra salary will result in a national insurance bill of £400 for the director personally (£3,336 x 12%). That's the bad news.

The good news is that, by increasing the director's salary from £8,164 to £11,500, £634 of additional corporation tax relief is obtained for the company (£3,336 x 19%).

The extra corporation tax relief outweighs the national insurance cost by £234.

Again this is not the end of the story. Where the directors withdraw the company's remaining profits as dividends the higher salary will use up the final £3,336 of their personal allowances, which means £3,336 of dividend income which would have been tax free will now typically be taxed at 7.5% or 32.5%.

On the plus side, the higher salary will reduce the amount of after-tax profit available to distribute as dividends by £2,702 (£3,336 less 19% corporation tax), which will reduce the dividend income on which the directors pay tax (typically at 7.5% or 32.5%).

The net effect of all this is that basic-rate taxpayers will typically save around £185 by taking a salary of £11,500 instead of £8,164 and many higher-rate taxpayers will typically save around £27.

In summary, for company owners with spare employment allowance, a salary of up to £11,500 will generally be more tax efficient than a salary of £8,164.

Salary over £11,500?

A company with no employees and two directors (e.g. a husband and wife) can pay the directors a salary of around £19,000 each with no employer's national insurance liability.

But is it worth paying salaries of more than £11,500 to avoid wasting the £3,000 employment allowance? From a strict comparison of tax bills the answer is typically no.

For example, if a salary of £19,000 is taken instead of £11,500 the additional income tax (at 20%) and employee's national insurance (at 12%) will outweigh the additional corporation tax relief (at 19%) by £975.

However, the £7,500 of additional salary will reduce the amount of after-tax profit available to distribute as dividends by £6,075 (£7,500 less 19% corporation tax), which will reduce the amount of dividend income on which the directors pay tax.

If the directors are basic-rate taxpayers, the income tax payable on their dividend income will fall by £456 (£6,075 x 7.5%). So overall they will be worse of by £519 (£975 - £456) by taking a salary of £19,000 instead of £11,500. Many may consider this a tax cost worth paying for the convenience of taking a larger salary without some of the restrictions and hassle that comes with paying dividends.

If the directors are higher-rate taxpayers, on the plus side they'll have £6,075 less dividend income taxed at 32.5%, saving them £1,974. Against this, the additional salary will use up £7,500 of their basic-rate bands which means they'll have £7,500 more dividend income taxed at 32.5% instead of 7.5%, costing them £1,875.

Overall many directors who are higher-rate taxpayers will be worse of by £876 (£1,974 - £1,875 - £975) by taking a salary of £19,000 instead of £11,500. Again, some may consider this a tax cost worth paying for the convenience of taking a larger sum of money out of their companies on a more regular basis.

In summary, for the 2017/18 tax year the most tax efficient salary for directors of companies with spare employment allowance is £11,500.

A director who takes an £11,500 salary will receive £11,100 after tax (£11,500 less £400 employee's national insurance).

Some directors may find it more convenient to take a slightly larger salary (e.g. £19,000) even if the tax cost is higher.

Is a Lower Salary Preferable?

Although a salary of £11,500 may be "optimal" for company owners with spare employment allowance, a lower salary may be preferable in some cases.

For example, if the company doesn't have any other employees, the directors may decide to pay themselves a salary of £8,164 each to avoid the hassle of having to make any national insurance payments (for example, to avoid late payment penalties).

Although a salary of £8,164 is completely tax free, it still has to be reported to HMRC as part of the normal payroll process (although it may be possible to make a single annual payroll submission in some circumstances – see Chapter 34).

It's also important to remember that there's a limit to the number of directors' salaries of £11,500 that can be paid before the £3,000 national insurance employment allowance is fully used up.

Higher Salaries

Although the salaries discussed in this chapter are "optimal" from a strict comparison of tax rates and thresholds, there may be other tax and non-tax reasons why you may wish to pay yourself a higher salary (see Part 7).

Chapter 8

Older & Younger Directors

Younger Directors

You can be a company director as long as you are 16 or older. When you turn 16 you also become subject to *employee's* national insurance.

However, if you are under 21 there is no *employer's* national insurance payable on your salary, as long as it does not exceed the higher-rate threshold (currently £45,000). Employer's national insurance is payable to the extent your salary exceeds £45,000.

For young directors, a salary of £11,500 is generally more tax efficient than a salary of £8,164 (for the same reason that it is more tax efficient when the company has spare employment allowance – see previous chapter).

Older Directors

If a company director is over state pension age there is no *employee's* national insurance payable on their salary.

Employer's national insurance is still payable, however.

For these older directors a salary of £11,500 is, at first glance, more tax efficient than a salary of £8,164.

However, as we shall see in Part 4, if you have income from other sources (including a state pension), you should take this other income into account when deciding how much salary to pay yourself.

In many cases, if employer's national insurance is payable, a salary of £8,164 will still be more tax efficient than a salary of £11,500.

National Insurance Free Salaries

A company director can receive a salary of more than £8,164 with no national insurance payable at all if:

- The director is over state pension age

- The company has spare employment allowance

It may be possible for a director in these circumstances to receive a salary of over £29,000 with no national insurance liability at all (for example, when there is just one other low-paid employee).

Where there are two directors over state pension age, and no other employees, it will be possible for the directors to receive salaries of around £19,000 each with no national insurance liability at all.

The only tax payable will be income tax at 20% once the director's personal allowance has been exhausted.

In some cases an overall saving of over £1,000 can be achieved by taking a larger national insurance free salary in preference to a smaller salary and dividends.

The only tax payable on the salary will be 20% income tax, compared with the combined 25% tax rate on dividend income once the dividend allowance has been exhausted – see Chapter 3).

Chapter 9

Salaries: Pension Benefits

Apart from being tax efficient a salary confers two extra benefits on the director/shareholder:

- State pension entitlement
- Ability to make private pension contributions

State Pension Entitlement

To protect your state pension entitlement you should pay yourself a salary that is greater than the national insurance 'lower earnings limit'.

For 2017/18, the lower earnings limit is £113 per week which requires a total annual salary of at least £5,876.

If you want to protect your state pension entitlement, a salary of at least £5,876 should be paid in 2017/18 in preference to taking dividends.

Private Pension Contributions

Everyone under the age of 75 can make a pension contribution of £3,600 per year. The actual cash contribution would be £2,880, with the taxman adding £720 to bring the total gross contribution to £3,600.

If you want to make bigger pension contributions the contributions you make *personally* (as opposed to contributions made by your company) must not exceed your 'relevant UK earnings'. Salaries count as earnings, dividends do not.

For a company director taking the "optimal" tax-free salary of £8,164, the maximum pension contribution he can make is £8,164.

This is the maximum *gross* contribution. The director would personally invest £6,531 (£8,164 x 0.8) and the taxman will top this up with £1,633 of basic-rate tax relief for a gross contribution of £8,164.

Similarly, a director taking a salary of £11,500 can make a maximum pension contribution of £11,500. The director would personally invest £9,200 (£11,500 x 0.8) and the taxman will top this up with £2,300 of basic-rate tax relief for a gross contribution of £11,500.

Company owners can also get their companies to make pension contributions, instead of making them personally. And as we shall see in Chapter 26, company pension contributions are currently more tax efficient than contributions made personally in many circumstances.

Chapter 10

Tax-free Dividends

If a company owner needs more income than the small "optimal" salary, as most probably will, the most tax-efficient solution is generally to take a dividend.

In this chapter we'll take a look at how much tax-free dividend income you can take and then in the next chapter we'll look at how much dividend income you can take taxed at just 7.5%.

We know from Chapter 3 that dividends attract no national insurance and are free from income tax to the extent they're covered by the director's personal allowance and £5,000 dividend nil rate band.

Companies with Employees
(i.e. with no spare employment allowance)

A director/shareholder who takes a tax-free salary of £8,164 and has no other income can take a tax-free cash dividend of £8,336. The first £3,336 will be covered by their remaining personal allowance and the final £5,000 will be tax free thanks to the dividend nil rate band.

Combined with the tax-free salary, this gives the director/shareholder the maximum total tax-free income for 2017/18 – £16,500:

- £8,164   Tax-free salary
- £8,336   Tax-free dividend

The Corporation Tax Bill

Although a dividend of £8,336 can be paid with no tax consequences for the director/shareholder, the payment is not completely tax free.

Dividends are paid out of a company's after-tax profits. So for a company that pays 19% corporation tax, a dividend of £8,336 will have a corporation tax bill of £1,955:

Pre-tax profits	£10,291
Less: corporation tax @ 19%	£1,955
After-tax profits/dividend	£8,336

So while dividends are tax efficient they are NOT tax free. This is an important point to remember, especially if you want to grow your business rather than extract income from it.

If, for example, a company incurs £10,291 of tax deductible expenditure before the end of its accounting period, its corporation tax bill will be reduced by £1,955. This will leave less after-tax profit to distribute as dividends but such a strategy may appeal to some business owners who would prefer to re-invest profits and minimise all taxes, including corporation tax.

The fact that dividends come with a corporation tax bill is why company owners should consider other profit extraction strategies, for example paying interest or making company pension contributions (Chapters 23 and 24). Some payments like these can be both tax free in the hands of the director and provide corporation tax relief. This is the best case scenario when it comes to extracting money from your company.

Having said this, most company owners need to extract additional cash from their companies every year to cover their living costs. This means some tax will usually always be payable, either by the company or the director personally. The key is to minimise it.

Finally, please note the corporation tax rate was reduced from 20% to 19% on 1 April 2017. Thus it's likely any dividend you receive this year will be paid out of profits that have been taxed at 20% or an effective rate of between 19% and 20% – see Chapter 1. We use the current 19% rate in most of the examples in this guide to keep things simple.

Companies with No Employees
(i.e. with spare employment allowance)

Company owners with no other income who decide to take a salary of £11,500 (because the company has spare employment allowance or because the director simply wants a larger salary) can take a tax-free dividend of £5,000.

Combined with an after-tax salary of £11,100 (£11,500 less £400 employee's national insurance), this gives the director/shareholder a total income of £16,100 in 2017/18:

- £11,100   After-tax salary
- £5,000   Tax-free dividend

Doubling the Tax-Free Income
(Companies owned by couples)

Many companies are started and run by married or unmarried couples.

For couples in business together, the salaries and tax-free dividends outlined above can be doubled up.

In other words, where salaries of £8,164 are taken:

Tax-free salaries	£16,328
Tax-free dividends	£16,672
Total tax-free income	£33,000

Where salaries of £11,500 are taken (£11,100 after tax):

Salaries	£22,200
Tax-free dividends	£10,000
Total income	£32,200

Spouses/Partners Brought into the Business

Of course, not all companies are started or managed by couples. In some cases the business may have been started before the couple met. In other cases, one member of the couple may not want to become actively involved in the business, for example if they have their own career or do not work at all.

In these cases the questions from a tax planning perspective are:

- Can a spouse/partner be employed in the business?

- Can shares in the company be transferred to a spouse/partner?

- How much tax will the above two strategies save?

We'll return to these important tax planning issues in Chapter 20.

Use it or Lose It!

A company owner may decide to not withdraw the maximum tax-free dividend for several reasons. However, it really is a case of use it or lose it: if you don't take the maximum tax-free dividend this year, you cannot take a bigger tax-free amount next year.

In fact, in April 2018 the dividend allowance will be reduced from £5,000 to £2,000, so company owners should make the most of the bigger allowance while they can!

Company Directors Tax Returns

Note that, even if you don't have any income tax to pay on your salary and dividends, you will still have to complete a tax return.

All company directors have this duty.

The Next Step: Taxable Dividends

The tax-free salaries and dividends listed above will not provide enough income for the vast majority of company owners, even if the amounts are doubled up where the company is owned by a couple. Those that require more income will have to pay income tax on any additional dividends withdrawn, as we shall now see.

Part 3

How to Extract More Income Tax Efficiently

Chapter 11

The Next Step:
Dividends Taxed at Just 7.5%

So far we've shown that a company owner who has no other income and takes a tax-free salary of £8,164 can also take a tax-free dividend of £8,336 for a total tax-free income of £16,500.

A company owner who takes a salary of £11,500 can take a tax-free dividend of £5,000 for a total income of £16,100 (net of employee's national insurance).

These amounts can be doubled up where the company is owned by a couple.

Of course, most company owners will require more income and the most tax-efficient route is normally to take a bigger dividend.

Any additional dividend income you take will be taxed, however as long as you keep your total income below the £45,000 higher-rate threshold you will pay just 7.5% income tax. If you take any more dividend income the tax rate jumps to 32.5%!

Salary of £8,164

If you've taken a salary of £8,164 and tax-free dividend of £8,336 the maximum amount of additional dividend income you can take taxed at just 7.5% is £28,500. The income tax payable on this additional dividend income will be £2,138.

In summary, you can take a salary of £8,164 and a total dividend of £36,836 for a total pre-tax income of £45,000. After paying £2,138 tax you'll be left with an after-tax income of £42,862.

These amounts can be doubled up if the company is owned by a couple, leaving them with a total after-tax income of £85,724 and a total tax bill of £4,276.

Salary vs Dividends

Even though the additional dividend is taxed, it is still much more tax efficient than taking a bigger salary.

To end up with the same after-tax income of £42,862, a director/shareholder would require an additional salary payment of £43,702, on top of the £8,164 already paid and the maximum tax-free dividend of £5,000.

Overall, the director would end up with the same amount of after-tax income but the company would end up with £8,448 less cash (because it has to make such a large salary payment to cover all the extra tax, especially national insurance).

The table below illustrates this effect in two companies: one paying a small salary and dividends, the other paying a big salary plus a £5,000 tax-free dividend.

In each case the director ends up with £42,862. The company paying the big salary ends up with £8,448 less cash.

	Small Salary £	Big Salary £
Company's tax		
Company profit	100,000	100,000
Less: Salary	8,164	51,866
Less: Employer's NI	0	6,031
Net Profit	91,836	42,103
Less: Corporation tax @ 19%	17,449	8,000
After-tax profit	74,387	34,103
Less: Dividend	36,836	5,000
Company cash	37,551	29,103
Director's tax		
Total income	45,000	56,866
Income tax	2,138	9,446*
National insurance	0	4,558
After-tax income	42,862	42,862

* £400 higher for Scottish taxpayers

Salary of £11,500

If you've taken a salary of £11,500 and tax-free dividend of £5,000 the maximum amount of additional dividend income you can take taxed at just 7.5% is £28,500. The income tax payable on this additional dividend income will be £2,138.

In summary, you can take a salary of £11,500 and a dividend of £33,500 for a total pre-tax income of £45,000. After paying £400 national insurance on your salary and £2,138 income tax on your dividend you'll be left with an after-tax income of £42,462.

These amounts can be doubled up if the company is owned by a couple, leaving them with a total after-tax income of £84,924 and a total tax and national insurance bill of £5,076.

Company Owners with Bigger Salaries

Of course not all company owners take a salary of £8,164 or £11,500. Some take a bigger salary because it suits them to do so, even if this is not the most tax efficient or "optimal" thing to do.

For example, a company owner who takes a salary of £30,000 can still take a tax-free dividend of £5,000 plus additional dividend income of up to £10,000 taxed at 7.5% (£45,000 - £30,000 - £5,000).

A company owner who takes a salary of £40,000 can still take a tax-free dividend of £5,000. However, because their total taxable income will be £45,000 any additional dividend income will be subject to tax at the higher rate of 32.5%.

Chapter 12

Making the Most of the 7.5% Tax Rate

So far we have shown that a company owner who takes a salary of £8,164 can receive dividend income of £8,336 tax free and a further £28,500 taxed at 7.5%.

A company owner who takes a salary of £11,500 can receive dividend income of £5,000 tax free and a further £28,500 taxed at 7.5%.

Company owners who extract more money from their companies will go over the £45,000 higher-rate threshold and start paying income tax at 32.5% on their dividends, which is a big leap!

(Remember, at this point, to keep things simple, we are assuming the company owner does not have any income from other sources.)

An important tax planning question is whether you should pay yourself as much dividend income as you can taxed at 7.5%, even if you don't need the money immediately?

It's impossible to provide a definitive answer to this question because every company owner is different. However, I will attempt to outline the main benefits and drawbacks in this chapter.

One of the main reasons why you may NOT want to pay yourself the maximum amount taxed at 7.5% this year is if you expect to be able to withdraw the same money tax free next year or in another tax year.

We've shown that a couple who take salaries of £8,164 each can also pay themselves tax-free dividends of £8,336 each – a total tax-free income of £33,000 in 2017/18. Unfortunately, the dividend allowance is being cut from £5,000 to £2,000 next year so it will no longer be possible to extract as much tax-free income.

Although some company owners may be able to survive on the tax-free amounts, most will not and will have to withdraw at least some dividend income each year taxed at 7.5%.

Arguably you then have fairly little to lose by withdrawing the maximum amount you can have taxed at 7.5% this year (£28,500).

The main drawback is you will end up paying income tax earlier than may be necessary. In other words, the extra money you pay in income tax will earn interest in the taxman's bank account instead of your company's bank account!

Most company bank accounts pay paltry amounts of interest at present so the potential loss is very small. Anything you lose can probably be more than made up by investing the extra dividend income in a cash ISA (the rates are typically far higher than for company bank accounts).

So what are the benefits of paying tax early? By paying yourself the maximum dividend taxed at 7.5% you stand to protect against:

- Further dividend tax increases
- Business risk
- Becoming a higher-rate taxpayer

It is possible (although by no means certain) that dividend tax rates will be increased again at some point in the future. Thus it may be better to withdraw as much income as you can taxed at 7.5% in case the rate is increased to, say, 10%.

Some company owners may also wish to remove surplus cash from their companies to protect against business risk (arguably your money is at greater risk in the company's bank account than your own).

It may also be worth paying yourself the maximum dividend taxed at 7.5% if you think you may become a higher-rate taxpayer in the future. In other words, it may be better to *definitely* pay 7.5% tax this year rather than *possibly* 32.5% in a future tax year.

Avoiding 32.5% Tax

Why would you expect to become a higher-rate taxpayer in the future? Perhaps you expect the profits of your business to grow significantly or you expect to receive more income from other sources, e.g. an inheritance.

Some landlords who were basic-rate taxpayers in the past will become higher-rate taxpayers as the tax relief on their finance costs is reduced from 2017/18 onwards. By the time we get to 2020/21 none of your buy-to-let interest will be tax deductible which means you may have significantly higher taxable rental profits. This in turn may push some or all of your dividend income over the higher-rate threshold where it will be taxed at 32.5% instead of 7.5%.

Although you may never become a higher-rate taxpayer, you arguably have very little to lose by paying yourself the maximum dividend taxed at 7.5%. If you do become a higher-rate taxpayer you'll save 25% (by paying 7.5% tax this year rather than 32.5% in the future). If you're wrong, you will lose nothing (because you will pay 7.5% tax this year rather than 7.5% in the future).

Reasons to Pay Smaller Dividends

A company owner may decide to not withdraw the maximum dividend taxed at 7.5% for several reasons:

- The company hasn't made enough profit
- The company needs the cash to grow
- The company owner doesn't need the money
- The company is forced to restrict its dividends
- The company owner has taxable capital gains

The Company Hasn't Made Enough Profit

The company doesn't need to have made any profit to pay *salaries* and tax-efficient salaries should be paid wherever possible because they are also a tax deductible expense and reduce the company's corporation tax bill (even if this is only at a later date if the company is currently not making profits). For example, a salary of £8,164 will reduce a company's tax bill by £1,551.

Dividends, on the other hand, can only be declared if the company has sufficient distributable profits.

It is not necessary for the company to actually make a profit in the year the dividend is paid, as long as there are sufficient accumulated profits (after tax) from previous years.

(See Chapter 34 for more information.)

The Company Needs the Cash to Grow

Even if the company has made sufficient profits, the directors may wish to hold onto the company's cash to grow the business.

If you prefer to retain the cash in your company, it may be possible for a dividend to be declared but not paid out. The dividend can simply be credited to the director's loan account and withdrawn at a later date when it is more convenient.

This may be more tax efficient than reducing dividends during one year and then declaring bigger dividends taxed at 32.5% in another year.

Note that the director will generally be subject to income tax on any dividend that has been declared but not paid out. In practice, this means that it may be necessary to pay out a portion of the dividend to help the director pay his tax bill.

The Company Owner Doesn't Need the Money

A company owner may decide to take a smaller dividend if he has other resources, such as inherited money or proceeds from selling another business or from selling other assets like property and shares. The company owner may also have a spouse/partner who earns enough income to support the family.

In these circumstances the company owner may believe it is sensible to limit the amount taken as dividends to avoid paying tax at 7.5%. In reality, the company owner may simply be storing up an income tax problem for the future. If accumulated profits are eventually paid out as a large dividend, an income tax charge of 32.5% or 38.1% could be payable on a significant portion of any dividend declared.

If income is withdrawn on a more regular annual basis, even if not required immediately, income tax can be restricted to 7.5%.

There is one important exception. If the company owner has taxable income from other sources, it may be prudent to take a smaller dividend. So far we have been assuming that the company owner has no other taxable income. If there is other taxable income that uses up some or all of the director's basic-rate band, it may be necessary to restrict dividends to avoid paying income tax at 32.5%. (More about directors with other income in Part 4.)

The Company is Forced to Restrict its Dividends

Lenders may place restrictions on dividend payments to protect their interests (i.e. to stop cash leaking out of the company that should be going to them). In these circumstances it may be difficult for the company owners to structure their dividend payments to mitigate tax.

The Company Owner Has Taxable Capital Gains

If you have taxable capital gains you may want to reduce the amount of income you withdraw from your company to free up some of your basic-rate band. This may allow you to pay less capital gains tax – see Chapter 38.

Alternatives to Dividends

Although paying tax at 7.5% is a lot better than paying tax at 32.5%, it's important to remember that dividends are paid out of income that has already been subjected to corporation tax.

Thus, if you are a basic-rate taxpayer, the true effective tax rate on your dividend income is 25%, not 7.5% (see Chapter 3).

This means dividends are now less tax efficient than certain other types of income that you may be able to extract from your company.

Take rental income for example. If your company pays you rent of £10,000 it can claim corporation tax relief, providing the rent is reasonable. If you're a basic-rate taxpayer you will pay 20% tax on the amount, leaving you with £8,000.

If, on the other hand, your company does not pay you rent it will have additional profits of £10,000 on which it will pay 19% corporation tax, leaving £8,100 to distribute as dividends. After paying 7.5% tax you will be left with £7,493.

Clearly, rental income is now a fair bit more tax efficient than dividend income in this situation (see Chapter 23 for more information).

I also suspect many directors will get their companies to make bigger pension contributions following the increase in dividend tax rates. If your company contributes £10,000 to your pension it can claim corporation tax relief, again providing the amount is reasonable. Ignoring investment growth, when you retire you will be able to withdraw 25% tax free and the rest will be taxed at 20% if you are basic-rate taxpayer (as most retirees are).

After tax you'll be left with £8,500, compared with £7,493 from a dividend (see Chapter 25 for more on pension contributions).

Clearly, there's a tension between paying dividends and other types of income. These other amounts will often be a tax deductible expense for the company which means they will reduce the company's profits and therefore the amount that can be paid out as dividend income in the future.

If a company has already realised profits and incurred corporation tax, arguably the most tax efficient thing to do is distribute the after-tax profits as a dividend, especially if it will be either tax free or taxed at just 7.5%.

However, paying dividends may also limit the financial resources available to the company to make other tax efficient payments during the current year, e.g. rental income and pension contributions.

Chapter 13

How to Avoid Paying
Tax at 32.5%

Summary So Far

So far we have shown that a company owner who takes a tax-free salary of £8,164 can extract a tax-free dividend of £8,336 and a £28,500 dividend taxed at 7.5%, leaving him with an after-tax income of £42,862.

A director/shareholder who takes a salary of £11,500 (£11,100 after national insurance) can extract a tax-free dividend of £5,000 and a £28,500 dividend taxed at 7.5%, leaving him with an after-tax income of £42,462.

In both scenarios the company owner ends up with a taxable income of £45,000 and is on the cusp of being a higher-rate taxpayer.

These amounts can be doubled in the case of companies owned and run by couples.

If you do not generally require more income, you may be able to adopt an 'income smoothing' strategy – taking the maximum tax-free salary and dividend plus the maximum dividend taxed at 7.5% every year where possible, regardless of whether the company has made bigger than normal profits or lower than normal profits.

Taking Bigger Dividends

If you want more income the optimal strategy is to take additional dividends rather than salary, in order to avoid the national insurance payable on employment income. However, now that you have reached the higher-rate threshold you will pay a whopping 32.5% income tax on any additional dividend income you take.

The next two income tax thresholds you have to watch out for are:

- £50,000   Child benefit tax charge
- £100,000   Personal allowance withdrawal

In this chapter we will assume that the company owner (or their spouse/partner) is not claiming any child benefit. We will return to child benefit in the next chapter.

In the absence of any child benefit being claimed, the next threshold to watch out for is £100,000, where your income tax personal allowance starts to be withdrawn. The personal allowance currently saves higher-rate taxpayers up to £4,600 in income tax, so many company owners will want to keep their income below £100,000 to avoid losing it.

Maximum Income

With total income of £45,000 the director can take an additional dividend of up to £55,000 taxed at 32.5% before the £100,000 threshold is reached.

A director who takes a salary of £8,164 and the rest of his income as dividends will be left with total after-tax income of £79,987:

£8,164 salary + £91,836 dividend - £20,013 tax = £79,987

A director who takes a salary of £11,500 (£11,100 after national insurance) will be left with a total after-tax income of £79,587:

£11,100 salary + £88,500 dividend - £20,013 tax = £79,587

If the company is owned and managed by a couple, the above amounts can potentially be doubled up.

Don't Forget the Corporation Tax Bill!

It's tempting to think that company owners who pay themselves any of the above amounts are paying relatively little tax. After all, a total of £100,000 is being extracted from the company with a total income tax bill of just £20,013. The effective income tax rate is just 20%!

However, it's important to remember that dividends are always paid out of a company's *after-tax* profits.

To pay a dividend of £91,836 the company will have had to make a profit of £113,378, resulting in a corporation tax bill of £21,542. Coupled with an income tax bill of £20,013, the total tax bill attached to the dividend is £41,555.

Alternatives to Dividends

In Chapter 3 I pointed out that, if you're a higher-rate taxpayer, the overall effective tax rate on your dividend income is now 45%. With the tax rate at this level, many small company owners may simply decide not to pay themselves any dividend income above the higher-rate threshold and will simply roll up cash inside their companies, possibly until the business is sold or wound up.

At this point it may be possible to pay just 10% capital gains tax on the funds extracted if the company owner qualifies for Entrepreneurs Relief. We'll explore this issue more in Chapter 28.

Other company owners may decide to pay themselves less dividend income and focus on other techniques to extract money from their companies, e.g. pension contributions.

For example, if your company contributes £10,000 to your pension it can claim corporation tax relief. Ignoring investment growth, when you retire you will be able to withdraw 25% tax free and the rest will be taxed at 20% if you are basic-rate taxpayer (as most retirees are).

After tax you'll be left with £8,500, compared with £5,468 if a dividend is taken instead and taxed at 32.5% (see Chapter 25 for more on pension contributions).

The increase in dividend tax rates could therefore backfire on the Government, which hopes to milk small company owners for hundreds of millions of pounds in the next few years. What they may discover is that the more you hike tax rates, the less tax you collect!

Postponing Dividends

If you want to extract more than £45,000 from your company it's worth remembering that the Government has promised to increase the higher-rate threshold to at least £50,000 by 2020/21.

By the time we get to 2020/21 you will hopefully be able to take an additional £5,000 of dividend income which will be taxed at 7.5% instead of 32.5%. Couples will therefore be able to withdraw at least £10,000 more dividend income *every year* taxed at 7.5% instead of 32.5%.

Some company owners may therefore decide to postpone some of their dividend income until the higher-rate threshold increases.

Sample Tax Bills

For company owners who want to withdraw more than £45,000 from their companies *this year*, Table 3 contains some sample income tax bills.

It's assumed that a tax-free salary of £8,164 or £11,500 is taken, with the remaining income taken as dividends. The table goes up to £100,000 – beyond that your income tax personal allowance is gradually withdrawn and you will face an additional tax sting.

The numbers in the table are fairly easy to calculate. The first £11,500 of income is tax free thanks to the personal allowance and the next £5,000 of dividend income is also tax free thanks to the dividend nil rate band.

The next £28,500 of dividend income is taxed at 7.5%, resulting in a tax liability of £2,138. At this point the company owner has income of £45,000 and is on the higher-rate threshold. Any additional dividend income will then be taxed at 32.5%. For example, someone who extracts income of £75,000 will pay £2,138 on the first £45,000 and £9,750 on the final £30,000 (£30,000 x 32.5%), resulting in a total income tax bill of £11,888.

In all cases the amounts listed in Table 3 can be doubled for companies owned and run by couples. For example, a couple can withdraw £100,000 (£50,000 each) with a total income tax bill of £7,526 (£3,763 each).

TABLE 3
Income between £45,000 and £100,000

Income £	Income Tax £	After-tax Income £
45,000	2,138	42,862
50,000	3,763	46,237
55,000	5,388	49,612
60,000	7,013	52,987
65,000	8,638	56,362
70,000	10,263	59,737
75,000	11,888	63,112
80,000	13,513	66,487
85,000	15,138	69,862
90,000	16,763	73,237
95,000	18,388	76,612
100,000	20,013	79,987

Notes:
1. Salary of £8,164 or £11,500 taken with rest of income as dividends
2. Where salary is £11,500 national insurance of £400 must also be included
3. For income over £45,000 the extra tax is simply 32.5% of the excess
4. Table may contains small rounding errors

Income Smoothing

If your company makes bigger than normal profits during one accounting period you may be tempted to pay yourself a bigger dividend, even if this results in income tax being payable at a higher rate on some of the dividend income.

Paying a bigger than normal dividend is perfectly acceptable from a tax planning perspective IF you expect the company's profits to remain at a higher level or continue to grow.

If, however, you expect the company's profits to fall back, it may be wiser to 'smooth' your income and withdraw any bumper profits gradually, paying tax at no more than 7.5%.

Chapter 14

How to Protect Your Child Benefit

If you want to withdraw more than £45,000 from your company *and* your household receives child benefit, the next income tax bracket you have to be aware of is £50,000-£60,000.

Child benefit is gradually withdrawn where any member of a household has over £50,000 income. This is done by imposing a High Income Child Benefit Charge on the highest earner in the household.

Once the highest earner's income reaches £60,000, all of the child benefit will effectively have been taken away in higher tax charges.

The £50,000 threshold can be increased or decreased by the Government but does not automatically increase with inflation. In other words, over time more and more taxpayers will end up paying the child benefit tax charge.

The child benefit charge has important implications for company owners who want to determine how much income to withdraw from their companies during the current and future tax years.

Child Benefit: How Much is it Worth?

Child benefit is an extremely valuable *tax-free* handout from the Government. Parents who qualify currently receive:

- £1,076.40 for the first child
- £712.40 for each subsequent child

Depending on the number of children, a family can expect to receive the following total child benefit payment:

Children	Total Child Benefit
1	£1,076
2	£1,789
3	£2,501
4	£3,214

plus £712.40 for each additional child

How Long Do Child Benefit Payments Continue?

Child benefit generally continues to be paid until your children are 16 years old.

The payments will continue until age 20 if the child is enrolled in full-time 'non-advanced' education, including:

- GCSEs
- A levels
- Scottish highers
- NVQ/SVQ level 1, 2 or 3
- BTEC National Diploma, National Certificate, 1st Diploma

So if your child is 16, 17, 18 or 19 and enrolled in one of the above courses, child benefit will continue to be paid.

Once the child is 20 years old all child benefit payments will cease.

The following courses do NOT qualify:

- Degrees
- Diploma of Higher Education
- NVQ level 4 or above
- HNCs or HNDs
- Teacher training

In other words, if your children are 16, 17, 18 or 19 and enrolled in any these courses, you will not receive any child benefit.

Total Value of Child Benefit

Child benefit payments continue for between 16 and 20 years. Based on current child benefit rates, the total amount you can expect to receive over the total period your child qualifies is:

- £17,222 to £21,528 tax free for the first child
- £11,398 to £14,248 tax free for each additional child

These are very much 'back of the envelope' figures because they ignore the potential danger that child benefit may not hold its real value if it doesn't increase in line inflation.

However, the figures clearly illustrate how valuable child benefit is over many years and why it's worth protecting where possible.

The £50,000 Threshold for Company Owners

To avoid the child benefit charge you have to keep your salary and dividends below £50,000.

In previous chapters we have shown that company owners can pay themselves income of up to £45,000 before becoming higher-rate taxpayers and paying 32.5% tax on their dividends.

This leaves you scope to pay an additional dividend of £5,000 before the child benefit charge comes into force. The total income tax payable on the additional dividend will be £1,625 (£5,000 x 32.5%).

Salary of £8,164

A company owner who takes a salary of £8,164 and wants to avoid the child benefit charge in 2017/18 can take a dividend of £41,836 (£8,336 will be tax free, £28,500 will be taxed at 7.5% and £5,000 at 32.5%). Total taxable income: £50,000. Total *after-tax* income: £46,237.

For a company owned and managed by a couple, the above amounts can be doubled up. Total after-tax income: £92,474.

Salary of £11,500

A company owner who takes a salary of £11,500 and wants to avoid the child benefit charge in 2017/18 can take a dividend of £38,500 (£5,000 will be tax free, £28,500 will be taxed at 7.5% and £5,000 at 32.5%). Total taxable income: £50,000. Total *after-tax* income: £45,837 (after also deducting £400 national insurance).

For a company owned and managed by a couple, the above amounts can be doubled up. Total after-tax income: £91,674.

Income between £50,000 and £60,000

If you want to extract more income from your company you will face paying the High Income Child Benefit Charge.

For every £100 of income over £50,000 a tax charge equivalent to 1% of the child benefit is levied on the highest earner in the household.

For example, if the highest earner in the household has income of £55,000, the tax charge will be equivalent to 50% of the child benefit claimed.

If the highest earner in the household has income of £60,000 or more, the tax charge will be 100% of the child benefit claimed.

For the highest earner in the household the child benefit charge creates the following marginal tax rates on dividend income in the £50,000-£60,000 tax bracket:

Children	Marginal Tax Rate on Dividends
1	43%
2	50%
3	58%
4	65%

Plus 7% for each additional child.

Example

David, a company owner, has taken a salary and dividends totalling £50,000 so far in 2017/18. He is the highest earner in a household claiming child benefit for two children.

David decides to withdraw additional dividend income of £10,000. His total income will be £60,000 so he will face the maximum child benefit charge. The tax payable on the additional dividend is £5,039, calculated as follows:

£10,000 dividend x 32.5%	*£3,250*
£1,789 child benefit x 100%	*£1,789*
Total additional tax	*£5,039*

The effective tax rate on the additional £10,000 dividend is 50.39%.

Income between £60,000 and £100,000

If your income is at least £60,000 you will already be paying the maximum child benefit charge. Income between £60,000 and £100,000 does not incur any further child benefit charge.

Dividends between £60,000 and £100,000 will continue to be taxed at 32.5%.

Once your income rises above £100,000 you face a fresh tax sting: withdrawal of the income tax personal allowance.

How to Avoid the Child Benefit Charge

Clearly taxpayers have an enormous incentive to escape the much higher tax rates that apply to dividends in the £50,000-£60,000 bracket.

Company owners may find it easier than other taxpayers to escape the child benefit charge because they can alter the amount of dividend income they receive each year. Some company owners may be able to avoid the charge altogether by keeping their income below £50,000.

Others, including those who usually withdraw more than £60,000 each year, may be able to avoid the charge in some tax years but not others, or partly reduce the charge.

Company owners can also spread their income among family members, for example, by gifting shares in the business to their spouses (see Chapter 20).

For the current and future tax years, the following dividend strategies could be considered:

Smooth Income

If the income you withdraw is currently somewhere between the higher-rate threshold (£45,000) and £50,000, and you expect your income to continue growing above £50,000, you could consider extracting approximately £50,000 for several tax years, where possible.

This may mean you pay yourself more income than you need to begin with and less income than you need later on, but by doing so you may be able to avoid the child benefit charge completely for several years.

Roller-Coaster Income

If you plan to withdraw *more than* £60,000 from 2017/18 onwards, you could consider taking big dividends during some tax years and smaller ones in other tax years.

For example, instead of taking £75,000 every year, consider taking £100,000 every second year, if possible, and £50,000 in the intervening years. This will allow you to avoid the child benefit charge every second year.

Similarly, a company owner who normally takes around £60,000 every year could consider taking £70,000 in year 1 and £50,000 in year 2, where possible.

Austerity

If your taxable income is normally over £50,000, you could consider keeping your income below £50,000 for several years to avoid the child benefit charge.

For example, let's say you have three children and your taxable income is normally around £60,000. If for the next three years you can afford to withdraw just £50,000, you may be able to protect over £7,500 of child benefit.

Other Issues

When paying yourself dividends that are smaller than normal or bigger than normal there may be lots of other issues to consider.

For example, you can only declare bigger dividends if the company has sufficient distributable profits.

If you postpone taking some of your dividends until a future tax year, you may leave yourself exposed to any future increase in tax on company owners. Remember tax rules are constantly changing.

If you take a smaller than normal dividend this may have other financial repercussions, for example it may affect the size of mortgage you are able to get.

Chapter 15

Income over £100,000

Summary So Far

So far we have shown that a director/shareholder of a company that has no spare employment allowance can extract a tax-free salary of £8,164 and a dividend of £91,836 (with £8,336 tax free, £28,500 taxed at 7.5% and £55,000 taxed at 32.5%). Total pre-tax income: £100,000. Total after-tax income: £79,987.

If the company has spare employment allowance, a salary of £11,500 can be taken with a total national insurance cost of £400. On top of this, a dividend of £88,500 can be taken (with £5,000 tax free, £28,500 taxed at 7.5% and £55,000 taxed at 32.5%). Total pre-tax income: £100,000. Total after-tax income: £79,587.

The above amounts can be doubled up if the company is also owned and run by your spouse/partner.

If the family is claiming child benefit, you may also have to watch out for the £50,000 threshold (see Chapter 14).

Income between £100,000 and £123,000

Many company owners will be satisfied with a net after tax income of over £79,000.

For those who wish to extract more cash, a dividend is often the best option. However, now you face an additional tax sting: withdrawal of your £11,500 income tax personal allowance.

Once your taxable income rises above £100,000, your personal allowance is gradually withdrawn. It is withdrawn at the rate of £1 for every £2 of additional income.

In other words, if you have income of £101,000 your personal allowance will be reduced by £500. Once your gross income reaches £123,000 you will have no personal allowance left at all.

Company owners with income in the £100,000-£123,000 bracket could end up paying income tax at an effective rate of over 50% on any additional dividends they withdraw.

Example
Annabel, a company owner, has already taken a salary of £8,164 and dividends of £91,836. Total income: £100,000. She decides to pays herself additional dividend income of £23,000. On the additional dividend she will pay 32.5% income tax: £7,475. She will also lose all of her personal allowance which means her salary of £8,164 will now be taxed at 20%. Additional tax: £1,633.

In addition, £3,336 of dividend income, previously covered by her personal allowance, will be taxed at 32.5%. Additional tax: £1,084. Finally, her salary uses up £8,164 of her basic-rate band which means £8,164 of dividends will be taxed at 32.5% instead of 7.5%. Additional tax: £2,041.

The total additional income tax is £12,233 which is equivalent to 53% of the £23,000 dividend.

Don't Forget the Corporation Tax Bill!

As always, it's important to remember that dividends are always paid out of a company's *after-tax* profits.

To pay an additional dividend of £23,000 the company will have had to make profit of £28,395, resulting in a corporation tax bill of £5,395. Coupled with an income tax bill of £12,233, the total tax bill on the £28,395 of profit is £17,628, i.e. 62%!

Income between £123,000 and £150,000

These extortionate tax rates do not apply to all dividend income over £100,000 – only income between £100,000 and £123,000.

Once your income exceeds £123,000 your personal allowance will have disappeared altogether and any additional dividends will be taxed at the regular rate applying to higher-rate taxpayers: 32.5%.

After that, the next threshold you have to watch out for is £150,000 where the additional rate of tax kicks in (see Chapter 16).

How to Avoid 53% Tax

Unlike regular salaried employees or owners of unincorporated businesses (sole traders and partnerships), company owners can avoid this extortionate tax rate by simply not paying themselves salary and dividends in excess of £100,000 per year.

In other words, a company owner taking a salary of £8,164 should extract dividends not exceeding £91,836 and a company owner taking a salary of £11,500 should extract dividends not exceeding £88,500.

A company owner whose income may fluctuate from year to year, in line with the company's profits, may want to consider smoothing income to avoid the £100,000 threshold. In other words, if possible try not to pay yourself a salary and dividend of £80,000 in year 1 and £120,000 in year 2. It may be better to pay yourself £100,000 during both tax years, to preserve your income tax personal allowance in year 2.

Bigger Companies

Owners of companies earning substantial profits face a dilemma. While they may choose to extract no more than £100,000 per year, ultimately they may end up with a lot of surplus cash inside their companies.

For example, if you are the only shareholder in a company that is making an after-tax profit of £200,000 per year, you may not wish to extract just £100,000 per year indefinitely, especially if the surplus cash is not needed to help grow the business.

Company owners who wish to pay themselves more than £100,000 per year may be able to occasionally preserve their personal allowances by adopting the 'roller-coaster' strategy: paying bigger dividends in some tax years and smaller dividends in other tax years.

Remember, once your income exceeds £123,000 your personal allowance will have disappeared altogether and there is no additional penalty for taking additional dividend income, providing you keep your income below £150,000.

For example, let's say you normally withdraw a salary of £8,164 and dividend of £111,836 (total income £120,000 per year). With this level of income most of your personal allowance will be withdrawn.

If instead you pay yourself income of £100,000 in year 1 and £140,000 in year 2, this will allow you to preserve your personal allowance in year 1. Potential tax saving: £3,408 (2017/18 tax rates).

Salary vs Dividends

If you intend to pay yourself one of the typical small salaries discussed in Chapter 7 (typically £8,164 or £11,500) and extract the rest of the company's profits as dividends, it *may* be possible to achieve a small additional tax saving by paying yourself an even smaller salary, if you expect to have taxable income of more than £100,000.

The potential tax savings depend on a number of factors, including how much profit the company makes and whether the company has spare national insurance employment allowance.

For example, where a company has spare employment allowance, the "optimal" salary for most company owners is £11,500. However, where a company owner's taxable income exceeds £100,000, it may be possible to achieve a tax saving of several hundred pounds by taking a salary equal to the £8,164 national insurance threshold instead.

In some cases a small further tax saving can be achieved by decreasing the salary even further but in other cases this will result in a *higher* tax bill – the interactions are complex!

Where a company does not have any spare employment allowance, the optimal salary for most company owners is typically £8,164. Again, in some cases a small tax saving can be achieved by taking a smaller salary but the potential tax saving is not very impressive (usually less than £100 in most cases, which is a very small saving for someone with so much income). In many other cases taking a smaller salary will result in a higher tax bill.

In summary, while a salary of £8,164 may be more tax efficient than a salary of £11,500 where the company owner has income of more than £100,000, reducing the salary further is probably not worth the fuss (unless you've done calculations specific to your personal circumstances which show that a further reduction is worthwhile).

When You Should Not Reduce Your Salary

There are also various tax and non-tax reasons why you may not want to reduce your salary. In other words, what may be 'mathematically optimal' does not always make for sound tax planning.

Pensions are a case in point. Anyone who wants to make a pension contribution higher than £3,600 (the minimum contribution that can be made by anyone under age 75) requires earnings. Salaries count as earnings, dividends do not.

Furthermore, in order to protect your state pension entitlement, you should always make sure you receive a salary that exceeds the national insurance 'lower earnings limit'. For 2017/18, the lower earnings limit is £113 per week which requires a total annual salary of at least £5,876.

When it comes to reducing your salary to achieve additional tax savings the permutations are too many to provide any simple guidelines here. Any analysis would have to be performed on a case by case basis.

Chapter 16

Income over £150,000

Once your income rises above £150,000 you become an 'additional rate' taxpayer. Most people are familiar with the 45% tax rate (previously 50%) that applies to most types of income above this threshold.

However, if you are a company owner it's likely it will be your dividends that take you over the £150,000 threshold (dividends are always treated as the top slice of income – see Chapter 17).

Once your dividend income rises above £150,000, the income tax rate rises from 32.5% to 38.1%.

Don't Forget the Corporation Tax Bill

Although 38.1% is lower than the 45% rate most people associate with income over £150,000, we must not forget that dividends are paid out of profits that have already been subject to corporation tax.

For example, if a company pays £190 corporation tax on £1,000 of profit, that leaves £810 to distribute as dividends. If the director/shareholder then pays 38.1% income tax on the £810 distribution, the additional tax comes to £309. The total tax paid by the director and the company is £499 which is 49.9%!

Will the Additional Rate Be Abolished?

David Cameron's Government once stated that the additional rate of tax was "temporary" (it came into effect just weeks before Gordon Brown was booted out of office).

However, when the rate was reduced from 50% to 45% in 2012 (36.1% to 30.6% for dividends), no date was given for a further reduction. Instead the Government backtracked and increased the additional rate for dividends to 38.1% in April 2016.

Although we are told that most Conservatives are ideologically committed to lower taxes, abolishing the additional rate would be politically difficult. The opposition parties would never stop banging on about "tax cuts for the rich".

In fact, I reckon the Government wouldn't have the bottle to reduce the additional rate even if there was overwhelming evidence that doing so would boost tax receipts and help tackle Public Enemy No. 1: the Budget deficit. Tax revenues apparently increased when the rate was cut from 50% to 45%, although the evidence is rather sketchy.

If Labour gets into power again there seems little doubt that the additional rate would be increased from 45% to at least 50%. What they would do to the dividend tax rate is unclear, however.

In Scotland the additional rate can be increased now that the Scottish Parliament has greater tax powers. However, the key thing to remember is that the Scottish Parliament can NOT tax dividend income, so many Scottish company owners would not be affected by any increase or decrease in the Scottish rate.

Avoiding the 38.1% Tax Rate

The simplest way to avoid paying 38.1% tax on your dividends is to keep your taxable income below £150,000 (e.g. by extracting higher than normal profits over more than one tax year). Fortunately, this is fairly simple for company owners to do because, unlike most other taxpayers, they can control their personal incomes to a large extent.

But owners of very profitable companies (who don't want to roll up profits inside the company indefinitely) should also remember that going over the additional-rate threshold is not as painful as going over the higher-rate threshold.

When your income rises above £45,000 the dividend tax rate goes from 7.5% to 32.5% and you start paying an extra £250 tax on every additional £1,000 of dividend income you receive. But when your income rises above £150,000 the dividend tax rate goes from 32.5% to 38.1% and you will pay just £56 more tax on every additional £1,000 of dividend income you receive.

Salary versus Dividends

From a strict comparison of tax rates, company owners who are additional-rate taxpayers may be able to save themselves a few pounds by not paying themselves any salary and taking all the company's profits as dividends.

Take a company that has profits of £250,000 and just one director/shareholder. If the owner pays himself a small tax-free salary of £8,164, the company will be left with profits of £195,887 to distribute as dividends (after paying 19% corporation tax). The company owner will then be left with £142,437 after paying income tax on his salary and dividends.

If he decides to take no salary and takes all the company's profits as dividends he will be left with £142,498, a total saving of £61.

Clearly the tax saving is miniscule for someone with this much income and, as has been pointed out before, there are other reasons why taking a salary may be desirable. For example, a salary of at least £5,876 this year is necessary for state pension purposes.

In fact, some company owners may desire a salary much larger than £8,164, even if this may not be strictly speaking "optimal". For example, if the company owner in the above example takes a salary of £30,000 instead of £8,164 and extracts the remaining profits as dividends, he will be £3,917 worse off overall. And if he takes a salary of £50,000 he will be £5,650 worse off overall.

Although these amounts are not insignificant, for someone with taxable income of more than £200,000 a loss of £5,650 is relatively small in *percentage* terms.

Similarly, if the owner of a company with profits of £500,000 pays himself a salary of £50,000 instead of £8,164 he will also be £5,650 worse off overall. His after-tax income will, however, fall by just 2% from £267,785 to £262,135.

The extra tax cost will, of course, be smaller if the company has spare employment allowance which reduces the employer's national insurance payable on the company owner's own salary.

TABLE 4
Tax Bills Compared
Company Owner vs Self Employed

Profits	Company Owner	Self-Employed	Extra Tax
£200,000	£82,632	£82,363	£269
£250,000	£107,563	£105,863	£1,699
£300,000	£132,493	£129,363	£3,130
£400,000	£182,354	£176,363	£5,991
£500,000	£232,215	£223,363	£8,852
£600,000	£282,076	£270,363	£11,713
£700,000	£331,937	£317,363	£14,574
£800,000	£381,798	£364,363	£17,435
£900,000	£431,659	£411,363	£20,296
£1,000,000	£481,520	£458,363	£23,157

Notes:
1. Company owner withdraws all the profits of the business
2. Company owner takes £8,164 salary and rest of income as dividends
3. Company owner tax bill includes 19% corporation tax and income tax
4. Self-employed tax bill includes income tax and national insurance

Using a Company versus Self-Employment

Most company owners probably realize that if they take all their income as salary, they could end up paying significantly more tax than a self-employed person (sole trader or partner) with the same income. This is because of the additional 13.8% employer's national insurance payable on most salary income.

It's interesting to note that, even if a company owner structures his pay in the most tax efficient manner, taking most or all of his income as dividends, he could still end up paying significantly more tax than a self-employed person. This situation will typically arise when the company owner withdraws most or all of the company's profits and is a high income earner.

Table 4 compares the total tax paid by a company owner (corporation tax and income tax) with the total tax paid by a self-employed business owner (income tax and national insurance) at different profit levels. In each case the business owners have over £150,000 of income and are additional-rate taxpayers.

For the company owner, it is assumed that a salary of £8,164 is taken (even though this is not necessarily "optimal") and all of the remaining after-tax profits are extracted as dividends.

The "extra tax" column is the additional tax paid by the company owner. For example, when profits are £500,000 a company owner will pay £8,852 more tax than a self-employed person.

This doesn't necessarily mean owners of companies with significant profits would be better off self-employed. If profits are kept inside the company to help it grow, the only tax payable will be corporation tax. Clearly paying just 19% corporation tax is a lot better than the 47% tax paid by self-employed people who are additional-rate taxpayers.

It is in these circumstances – when profits are reinvested – that companies are most powerful as tax shelters. For example, where a company has profits of £500,000 and only half the after-tax profits are paid out as dividends, the total tax bill will be around £67,000 less than the tax paid by a self-employed person.

Alternative Profit Extraction Strategies

Many company owners may wish to keep their total income below £150,000 by adopting various alternative profit extraction strategies, including:

- Gifting shares in the business to family members, including family members who are higher-rate taxpayers (see Part 5)

- Making personal or company pension contributions (see Chapters 25 and 26)

- Keeping cash inside the company until the business is sold or wound up (see Chapter 28). At this point it may be possible to pay just 10% capital gains tax on the extracted funds

Pension Contributions

Additional-rate taxpayers typically enjoy 45% tax relief on their pension contributions but the amount they can invest is restricted.

For starters, company owners who pay themselves small salaries can only make small pension contributions personally (your pension contributions cannot exceed your earnings and dividends don't count as earnings).

For example, if you pay yourself a salary of £8,164 in 2017/18 you can only make a pension contribution of £8,164 personally (£6,531 contributed by you, with a further £1,633 added to your pension by the taxman).

Company owners who wish to make bigger pension contributions can either pay themselves higher salaries or get their companies to make the contributions on their behalf.

A higher salary may come with a punitive national insurance bill, so company pension contributions are often the preferred route.

Company pension contributions enjoy corporation tax relief, providing they are not excessive (see Chapter 26).

The Pension Taper

High income earners face another restriction on the amount that can be invested in their pensions. The annual allowance (normally £40,000) is reduced if your "adjusted income" exceeds £150,000.

Broadly speaking, your adjusted income is your total taxable income plus any pension contributions made by your employer (this is to prevent employees giving up salary in exchange for employer pension contributions to avoid the cap).

You must also add back any contributions you've made to an occupational pension scheme under a net pay arrangement (where employee contributions are deducted by the employer before calculating tax under PAYE).

The annual allowance is reduced by £1 for every £2 your income exceeds the £150,000 threshold. For example, an individual with adjusted income of £160,000 will have an annual allowance of £35,000 (£40,000 - £10,000/2).

The annual allowance cannot fall below £10,000 – this is the minimum amount that everyone affected by the taper can contribute to a pension.

Pension contributions that exceed the tapered annual allowance are added to your income and taxed (possibly at 45% if you are an additional-rate taxpayer). If the charge exceeds £2,000 you may instead have the charge deducted from your pension scheme.

Threshold Income

Note that if your "threshold income" is £110,000 or less you are exempt from tapering and can make pension contributions just like anyone else.

Your threshold income is, broadly speaking, your total taxable income less any pension contributions you have made personally.

Employer pension contributions are ignored when calculating threshold income. But you must add back any salary sacrificed in exchange for employer pension contributions after 8 July 2015.

Broadly speaking, adjusted income includes all pension contributions (including any employer contributions) while threshold income excludes pension contributions.

Example

Mario is a company owner with taxable income of £100,000. He gets his company to make a £60,000 pension contribution (carrying forward unused annual allowance). His adjusted income is £160,000 but his threshold income is £100,000, so his annual allowance is not reduced.

Calculating the Tapered Annual Allowance in Practice

Company owners will find it fairly easy to calculate their adjusted and threshold income when it comes to salaries and dividends.

They should also find it relatively easy to reduce the amount of income they extract from their companies in order to stay below these thresholds and make full use of the maximum £40,000 annual allowance.

However, problems may arise when the company owner has other income that is less predictable, for example rental income from properties. Company owners who are also landlords may not know precisely how much taxable income they have earned (and thus their tapered annual allowance) until *after* the tax year has ended. By then it will be too late to make pension contributions.

Those who wish to benefit from pension contributions and think they may be affected by the tapered annual allowance may therefore need to estimate their total taxable income just *before* the end of the tax year.

The Tapered Annual Allowance and Carry Forward

Fortunately, all is not lost if your pension contributions exceed your tapered annual allowance for the year. Those affected by the tapered annual allowance can still carry forward any unused annual allowance from the three previous tax years.

Carry forward could therefore act as a lifeline for those whose pension contributions accidentally exceed the tapered annual allowance in any given year.

For example, if your annual allowance last year (2016/17) was reduced from £40,000 to £30,000 and you made a £20,000 pension contribution, you will have £10,000 left to carry forward to the current year (£30,000 - £20,000).

The taper did not apply before 2016/17 so it is possible you will have up to £40,000 of unused annual allowance from each of the 2014/15 and 2015/16 tax years to use this year.

Part 4

Company Owners with Income from Other Sources

Chapter 17

Keeping Income Below the Key Thresholds

Introduction

In Chapter 6 we explained why company owners, when deciding how much income to withdraw from their companies, need to be aware of the following income tax thresholds and brackets:

- Over £45,000   Higher rate tax
- £50,000-£60,000   Child benefit tax charge
- £100,000-£123,000   Personal allowance withdrawal
- Over £150,000   Additional rate of tax

If your total taxable income is less than £45,000 you'll pay no more than 7.5% income tax on your dividends. Once your income exceeds £45,000, you start paying tax at 32.5%.

However, dividend income that falls into the final three tax brackets is taxed at much higher rates:

- £50,000-£60,000   43% to 65% or more
- £100,000-£123,000   53% in some cases
- Over £150,000   38.1%

(Note: the £50,000-£60,000 threshold only applies to households in receipt of child benefit.)

When trying to avoid these extortionate tax rates, you must remember to include any other taxable income you receive. If you have taxable income from other sources it may force your company income, in particular your dividend income, into a higher tax bracket.

To avoid a potential tax sting you may wish to reduce the amount of income you withdraw from your company or take other steps to reduce your tax bill.

The Order in which Income is Taxed

Income is taxed in the following order:

- Non-savings income:
  - ➢ Employment income
  - ➢ Self-employment income
  - ➢ Rental income
- Savings income
- Dividend income

Dividends are always treated as the top slice of income.

Let's say you expect to earn £10,000 of rental income during the current tax year but, so far, have not withdrawn any income from your company. As things stand, all of your rental income will be tax free, being covered by your income tax personal allowance.

Let's say you now decide to withdraw a salary of £11,500 and a dividend of £33,500 from your company (the maximum amount you can withdraw tax free or taxed at just 7.5%, in the absence of any other income).

The decision to take a salary means you now have £21,500 of non-savings income and your income tax bill will increase by £2,000:

£21,500 - £11,500 personal allowance = £10,000 x 20% = £2,000

Effectively, you've paid 20% tax on your salary.

And what about your dividends which are supposedly taxed at no more than 7.5%?

Thanks to your rental income, £10,000 of your dividend income will now be pushed into the higher-rate tax bracket and taxed at 32.5% instead of 7.5%, resulting in additional tax of £2,500.

In summary, having £10,000 of rental income increases the company owner's tax bill by £4,500!

Income from Other Sources

With the exception of self-employment income, it may be possible to extract all of the various types of income listed above from your own company: employment income, rental income, interest income, and dividend income.

We've already talked extensively about salaries (employment income) and dividends. If your company uses a property that you own personally (for example, an office or shop) it can also pay you rent; and if your company borrows money from you it can pay you interest.

In Chapters 23 and 24 we take a look at whether it is tax efficient to get your company to pay you rent or interest and how much.

In this part of the guide the focus is on company owners who have income from *other sources* – i.e. income that does not come out of their own company.

More specifically, the focus is on company owners who have income from other sources that is subject to *income tax*.

Some income (e.g. most interest income and stock market dividends) can be sheltered from income tax inside an ISA or pension scheme.

It is also possible to shelter assets from income tax inside another company. Some property investors do this. Corporation tax is still payable on any rental profits produced by the properties but the income tax position of the director/shareholder will be unaffected, unless those profits are extracted.

Those company owners who do have a significant amount of taxable income from other sources, and cannot shelter it from income tax, may wish to reduce the amount of income they withdraw from their own companies, so as to avoid paying income tax at some of the extortionate rates listed at the beginning of this chapter.

Other Income – Control

One of the benefits of being a company owner is you can control how much income you withdraw from your business. This allows you to control your income tax bill from year to year.

Income from other sources is often less easy to control. For example, it may not be possible to shift it from one tax year into another tax year. You may be able to control the dividends declared by your own company but you cannot force the board of Vodafone to increase or lower its dividend!

Company owners who want to keep their taxable income just below any of the key income tax thresholds may therefore have to increase or decrease their *company income* – it may not always be possible to alter the amount of income you receive from other sources.

Table 5 shows the maximum dividend you can withdraw during 2017/18 if you have other taxable income (including employment income) and want to avoid some of the key income tax thresholds.

For example, if you have other taxable income of £20,000 a dividend of £25,000 will keep your income below £45,000 and you will avoid paying 32.5% tax.

A dividend of up to £30,000 will ensure that your income does not exceed £50,000. Some of your dividend income will be taxed at 32.5% but you will avoid the child benefit tax charge.

A dividend of up to £80,000 will ensure that your income does not exceed £100,000. A significant amount of your dividend income will be taxed at 32.5% and you may end up paying the maximum child benefit tax charge but you will not lose any of your personal allowance.

TABLE 5
Avoiding the Tax Thresholds
Maximum Dividend 2017/18

Other Income	Threshold		
	£45,000	£50,000	£100,000
£8,164	£36,836	£41,836	£91,836
£11,500	£33,500	£38,500	£88,500
£15,000	£30,000	£35,000	£85,000
£20,000	£25,000	£30,000	£80,000
£25,000	£20,000	£25,000	£75,000
£30,000	£15,000	£20,000	£70,000
£35,000	£10,000	£15,000	£65,000
£40,000	£5,000	£10,000	£60,000
£45,000	£0	£5,000	£55,000
£50,000	£0	£0	£50,000

Note: Table may contain small rounding errors

Other Income – Predictability

At the start of a new tax year you may not know with complete certainty how much taxable income you will receive from other sources during the year. This could be problematic if you wish to withdraw dividends from your company *at the beginning of the tax year*.

If you withdraw dividends from your company and your other income then turns out to be higher than expected, you may end up paying more income tax than you expected on your company dividends.

Some types of income are, however, more predictable than others. For example, interest income, stock market dividends and rental income are arguably more predictable than, say, the profits of a sole trader business (self-employment income).

Some types of income, if not completely predictable, are more likely to end up being *less than expected*, rather than higher than expected. For example, a rental property that normally generates rental income of £1,000 per month may lie empty for three months, thereby producing an annual income of £9,000 rather than £12,000.

If your income from other sources turns out to be less than expected, you may be able to get your company to pay you additional dividend income before the end of the tax year.

If your income from other sources turns out to be *higher than expected* you generally cannot reverse any dividends you have already taken out of your company, although it may be possible to do some emergency year-end tax planning (see Chapter 19).

Company owners who have unpredictable income from other sources may therefore wish to postpone paying dividends until closer to the end of the tax year, if they are concerned that their dividend income may fall into a heavily taxed bracket.

Scottish Company Owners

Table 5 is also relevant to company owners who live in Scotland and have income from other sources.

At present the only difference between Scotland and the rest of the UK is the higher-rate threshold, which is £43,000 in Scotland and £45,000 in the rest of the UK. However, the £45,000 threshold still applies to dividend and interest income.

To understand what this means in practice, picture a Scottish company owner who has three types of income: salary, rental income and dividends.

If his salary and rental income is less than £43,000 he will pay exactly the same amount of tax on ALL his income as taxpayers in the rest of the UK.

For example, if his salary and rental income total £35,000 he can receive dividend income of £10,000 before becoming a higher-rate taxpayer and paying 32.5% tax on his dividends.

If his salary and rental income is more than £45,000 he will pay exactly the same amount of tax on his dividend income as taxpayers in the rest of the UK. The only difference is he will pay an extra £400 tax on his salary and rental income.

Chapter 18

Should I Pay Myself a Smaller Salary?

So far we have shown that, if you have income from other sources, you may wish to reduce your company *dividends* to avoid various tax thresholds.

Another important question is: "Should I pay myself a smaller salary?"

If you intend to pay yourself one of the small salaries discussed in Chapter 7 (typically £8,164 or £11,500) and extract the rest of the company's profits as dividends, it may be possible to increase your after-tax disposable income by reducing your company salary in some circumstances.

For example, in Chapter 7 it was shown that, where a company has spare national insurance employment allowance, the optimal salary for most company owners is £11,500.

However, where the company owner has taxable income from other sources, it may be possible to achieve a tax saving of a few hundred pounds by taking a salary equal to the £8,164 national insurance threshold instead.

In Chapter 7 it was also shown that, where a company has employees and does not have any spare employment allowance, the optimal salary for most company owners is £8,164.

Where the company owner has taxable income from other sources (e.g. rental income) in most cases a tax saving will NOT be achieved by taking a salary smaller than £8,164.

A smaller salary may, however, be preferable when the company owner wishes to extract just a small amount of income in total from the company. This is because, if you have other income that uses up your personal allowance, the "optimal" salary/dividend profit extraction strategy is typically as follows:

- First, pay yourself any dividend which is tax free thanks to your dividend allowance (currently £5,000)

- Second, pay yourself a salary up to the national insurance threshold (currently £8,164)

- Pay any further amounts as dividends

The reason a tax-free dividend is the first port of call is because the only tax payable is corporation tax, currently at a rate as low as 19%.

By contrast, if you have other income that uses up your personal allowance, any salary you pay yourself will effectively be taxed at a rate of 20%. And if your other income also uses up your basic-rate band, any salary you pay yourself will effectively be taxed at 40%.

So a tax-free dividend is better than salary in these circumstances.

If you want to extract more than your £5,000 tax-free dividend a salary of up to £8,164 is generally the best option because there will be no national insurance and income tax will be payable at the 'regular' rates, typically 20% or 40%, compared with the combined tax rates on additional dividend income of 25% or 45% – see Chapter 3.

Once you've taken a salary of £8,164, dividends are generally better than salary because any additional salary you pay yourself will be subject to national insurance.

What all this means is that, if you wish to extract less than £13,164 (£5,000 + £8,164) a salary of less than £8,164 may be optimal.

But if you wish to extract more than £13,164 a salary of £8,164 is generally optimal, with the rest of your income taken as dividends – the same profit extraction strategy that applies to company owners who do not have other income, as discussed in previous chapters.

Having said all this, there are lots of reasons why you may not wish to reduce your salary or why it may not be practical to reduce your salary:

- To keep your earnings above the lower earnings limit (£5,876 in 2017/18) to protect your state pension entitlement (See Chapter 9).

- To make bigger pension contributions personally (see Chapter 26).

- Because your income from other sources may not be known at the beginning of the year, when you may wish to start making monthly salary payments.

- Because the taxman may question any reduction in your salary (see Chapter 36).

Chapter 19

The Different Types of Income

Let's take a closer look at the different types of income you may earn from other sources and how they may affect the income you decide to withdraw from your own company:

Employment Income

It is possible to have more than one source of employment income, for example:

- Salary from a second job with a separate employer, or
- Salary from a second company you own

If you have recently started out in business, it is possible that you will have a second job (possibly a part-time job) to help pay the bills.

If you start a second company to house a separate business venture there is, of course, nothing to stop you paying yourself a second salary.

For income tax purposes you are only entitled to one personal allowance (£11,500 in 2017/18). This generally means that you can only have one tax-free salary (unless, of course, the two salaries, when added together, total less than £11,500). Some or all of the second salary may be taxed at 20%.

National insurance is generally calculated differently. Employees who have more than one small salary (less than £8,164 in 2017/18), may not have to pay national insurance contributions at all. This is because the earnings from each job may be treated separately.

If the two businesses are in association, however, the salaries will be added together and national insurance may be payable.

Employers are considered to be in association if:

- The businesses serve a common purpose, and

- There is significant sharing of things like premises, personnel, equipment or customers

Following the increase in dividend tax rates, a second salary may be more tax efficient than a dividend in certain circumstances, providing there is no national insurance payable.

If you wish to pay yourself two salaries it may be necessary to obtain professional advice to satisfy yourself that the companies will not be treated by HMRC as being in association, with resulting national insurance liabilities.

Finally, there may, of course, be other tax and non-tax reasons why you wish to pay yourself a second salary or a bigger second salary.

Self-Employment Income

You may have self-employment income if you have another business that is not a company (i.e. you're a sole trader or belong to a partnership). Many entrepreneurs have multiple businesses and it's possible a second or third business will not be a company.

Companies can be wonderful tax shelters but unincorporated businesses have advantages of their own, including lower accountancy fees, more generous treatment of certain expenses and more generous capital allowances for cars used in the business.

Self-employment income may be difficult to predict – especially close to the beginning of a new tax year – making it difficult to decide how much income to withdraw from the company business.

Fortunately, as far as your self-employment business is concerned, it may be possible to do some emergency year-end tax planning to reduce its taxable profits (e.g. by making pension contributions or incurring other tax deductible expenditure).

Rental Income

When we use the term 'rental income' what we mean is rental *profit*. You may receive rents of £10,000 per year but your rental profits may only be £5,000, after deducting all the expenses property investors can claim.

Unlike interest income and stock market dividends, most rental income cannot be sheltered from income tax in an ISA, pension scheme or other tax shelter.

There are, however a couple of exceptions:

- Commercial property held in a pension scheme

- Residential or commercial property held in a company

Some business owners place their trading premises inside a self-invested personal pension (SIPP) to avoid income tax and capital gains tax (see Chapter 27).

Others put their properties in a separate company. Corporation tax is payable on the company's income and capital gains but your own income tax bill will be unaffected, unless the property company's profits are extracted.

Apart from these two exceptions, most landlords own their properties *personally*, which means they are fully exposed to income tax on their rental profits. These rental profits may then need to be factored into the mix when deciding how much income you withdraw from your company.

For example, in 2017/18 if you take a salary of £8,164 and expect to have taxable rental profits of £20,000 you can take tax-free dividend income of £5,000 plus additional dividend income of £11,836 taxed at 7.5%. This takes you up to the £45,000 higher-rate threshold. Any additional dividend income you receive will be taxed at 32.5%.

If you take a salary of £8,164 and expect to have taxable rental profits of £40,000 you can still take tax-free dividend income of £5,000 (because everyone can benefit from the dividend nil rate band). However, any additional dividend income will be taxed at 32.5%.

Rental losses

If you have rental losses brought forward from previous years you will not have to pay any income tax on the rental profit you make during the current tax year (providing, the loss brought forward is big enough to completely offset the current year's profit).

If the rental profit you make during the current tax year is not taxable it does not need to be factored into the mix when deciding how much income you withdraw from your company.

Changes to Mortgage Tax Relief

Tax relief for interest and finance costs paid by individual landlords who own residential properties is now being restricted.

The new rules do not apply to commercial properties or furnished holiday lettings or to properties held inside companies.

Tax relief is currently being phased out over a period of four years and replaced with a 20% basic-rate "tax reduction" as follows:

- 2017/18   75% deducted as normal, 25% at basic rate only
- 2018/19   50% deducted as normal, 50% at basic rate only
- 2019/20   25% deducted as normal, 75% at basic rate only
- 2020/21   All relieved at basic rate only from this year on

Thus, company owners who have a separate rental property business have to contend with two major tax changes:

- Higher tax rates for dividends (2016/17 onwards)
- Reduced tax relief on mortgage interest (2017/18 onwards)

The reduced tax relief on mortgage interest means many landlords will have bigger taxable rental profits.

This in turn will push more of the dividend income they receive from their companies over the higher-rate threshold where it will be subject to the new 32.5% tax rate.

Example

It's 2020/21 and we will assume the personal allowance has been increased to £12,500 and the higher-rate threshold to £50,000.

Sinead owns a graphic design company and pays herself a tax-free salary of £12,500 and dividends of £40,000.

She's also a landlord and earns a rental profit of £35,500 before deducting her interest costs. She pays £12,000 interest on her buy-to-let mortgages, so her true rental profit is £23,500. However, with her mortgage interest no longer tax deductible, her taxable rental profit will be £35,500. Along with her salary of £12,500 this will take her income up to £48,000.

Because this is still below the £50,000 higher-rate threshold all of her taxable rental profit will be taxed at 20%, with an offsetting tax reduction of 20% of her mortgage interest. So at first glance it looks like she is unaffected by the change to interest tax relief.

Where Sinead will feel the sting, however, is on her dividend income. Dividends are always treated as the top slice of income. The first £2,000 of her dividend income will be tax free thanks to the dividend nil rate band but this will take her income up to the £50,000 higher-rate threshold.

All of her remaining dividend income will therefore be taxed at the 32.5% higher rate.

The end result is that, because her taxable rental profits increase by £12,000, this will push £12,000 of her dividend income over the higher-rate threshold where it will be taxed at 32.5% instead of 7.5% – an increase of 25%.

Thus her final tax bill will increase by £3,000 (£12,000 x 25%).

Many company owners who are also landlords will find themselves in a similar position and will see their tax bills increase by an amount equivalent to 25% of their mortgage interest.

For example, a company owner with £20,000 of buy-to-let interest could end up paying £5,000 more tax in 2020/21.

Tax Planning for Landlords

Company owners who are also landlords with mortgages should consider paying themselves as much dividend income as they can taxed at 7.5% over the next few years if they think the tax relief restriction will force them to pay 32.5% tax in the future.

Example
Jessie owns a small engineering company and pays herself a salary of £11,500 which is tax free thanks to her personal allowance (ignoring a small amount of national insurance).

She also owns a couple of rental properties and earns rental income of £24,000 (net of all expenses except interest) and pays £14,000 interest on her buy-to-let mortgages. To keep things simple we'll assume her rental income and expenses stay the same for the next few years.

During the current 2017/18 tax year three quarters of her finance costs are tax deductible so she will have a taxable rental profit of £13,500.

This means she can pay herself a dividend of up to £20,000 before she becomes a higher-rate taxpayer and has to pay 32.5% tax (£45,000 - £11,500 - £13,500). The first £5,000 will be tax free and the remainder will be taxed at 7.5%.

By the time we get to 2020/21 the personal allowance and higher-rate threshold are expected to be at least £12,500 and £50,000 respectively. None of Jessie's finance costs will be tax deductible so she will have a taxable rental profit of £24,000.

Assuming she pays herself a salary of £12,500, this means she can pay herself a dividend of up to £13,500 before she becomes a higher-rate taxpayer and has to pay 32.5% tax (£50,000 - £12,500 - £24,000).

In summary, the maximum amount of dividend income Jessie can extract from her company taxed at no more than 7.5% is £20,000 this year and will gradually fall to £13,500 in 2020/21.

She should consider paying herself these "maximum amounts" between now and 2020/21, even though she may not need the income immediately.

Interest Income

Most interest income can be sheltered from tax inside an ISA or SIPP. Other tax-free investments include index-linked savings certificates (when they're available) and offset mortgages (instead of earning interest, your savings are used to reduce the interest on your mortgage). Even paying off personal debts is effectively a way to earn tax-free interest.

Wealthier individuals, with large cash balances or holdings of corporate and government bonds may, of course, have a significant amount of taxable interest income and there may also be times in life when less wealthy taxpayers have significant amounts of taxable interest income:

- You sell your home and have a large cash lump sum
- You lend money to a friend or family member
- You receive a big dividend and put the cash in the bank
- You lend money to your company (see Chapter 24)

This income may need to be factored into the equation when you decide how much income to withdraw from your company.

The £5,000 Starting Rate Band

When it comes to interest income, many company owners are in a fortunate position. They can receive up to £5,000 of interest *tax free* each year thanks to the 0% starting-rate band.

The starting rate is supposed to benefit only those with very low incomes. Hence the £5,000 starting rate band is reduced by any other taxable *non-savings* income you have including:

- Employment income
- Self-employment income
- Pension income
- Rental income

If your taxable non-savings income exceeds the £5,000 starting rate band, none of your interest income will be covered by the starting rate band.

Of course, most regular salary earners and self-employed business owners will have more than £5,000 of taxable non-savings income. Many company owners are in a different position, however. Note that the above list of non-savings income does NOT include dividends. Dividends are the top slice of income and do not use up the starting rate band.

Because company owners often pay themselves small salaries and take the rest of their income as dividends, they will often have little or no taxable non-savings income. As a result, many can earn at least £5,000 of tax-free interest!

Example
Mandy is a company owner with a salary of £11,500, dividend income of £28,500 and interest income of £5,000. Her salary is tax free thanks to her personal allowance and she therefore has no taxable non-savings income that uses up her starting rate band (her dividend income does not count). Her interest income is fully covered by her £5,000 starting rate band and taxed at 0%.

Many company directors will thus pay 0% tax on their interest if:

- They take a small salary from their company,
- Do not have a sole trader or partnership business, and
- Don't earn much, if any, rental income.

It is important to point out that the 0% starting rate band is not given in addition to your basic-rate band (£33,500 in 2017/18). Instead it is part of your basic-rate band.

If you qualify to use the starting rate band your basic-rate band will be reduced, possibly pushing some of your dividend income into a higher tax bracket.

The New Savings Allowance

The savings allowance (also known as the savings nil rate band) came into effect on 6 April 2016 and exempts from tax up to £1,000 of interest income for basic-rate taxpayers and up to £500 for higher-rate taxpayers. Additional rate taxpayers cannot benefit from the savings nil rate band.

As part of these reforms, the automatic deduction of 20% income tax by banks and building societies has now ceased.

The savings nil rate band operates separately from, and in addition to, the starting rate band. This means some company owners can earn up to £6,000 of tax-free interest every year (over and above any income that is covered by the personal allowance).

Income that falls within the savings nil rate band uses up some of the band that it falls into. For example, if you have £44,500 of salary and rental income and £1,000 of interest income you will have total income of £45,500.

As a higher-rate taxpayer you will therefore be entitled to a £500 savings nil rate band. Thus £500 of your interest income will be tax free and this will use up the final £500 of your basic-rate band. The final £500 will be taxed at 40%.

The savings nil rate band will be useful to company owners who cannot use the starting rate band because they have too much non-savings income, e.g. rental income. Most can now enjoy £1,000 or £500 of tax-free interest. It may also be useful for extracting interest from your own company (see Chapter 24).

Interest Income - Examples

The somewhat complex operation of the starting rate band and savings nil rate band is best explained with some examples:

Example
Samantha is a company owner with a salary of £11,500 and interest income of £5,000. She also has £10,000 of rental income.

Her salary is covered by her personal allowance but thanks to her rental income she has £10,000 of taxable non-savings income. Because her taxable non-savings income exceeds the £5,000 starting rate limit, none of her interest income is covered by the 0% starting rate.

However, because she is a basic-rate taxpayer (her total income is less than £45,000) she is entitled to a £1,000 savings nil rate band. So £1,000 of her interest income will be tax free, the remaining £4,000 will be taxed at 20%.

Example

Elaine is a company owner with a salary of £8,000, rental income of £8,000, interest income of £1,000 and dividends of £20,000 (total income £37,000).

There is no income tax on her salary and the first £3,500 of her rental income is covered by her remaining personal allowance. The final £4,500 of her rental income is taxed at 20% and uses up £4,500 of her starting rate band. Thus £500 of her interest income is covered by her remaining starting rate band.

As a basic-rate taxpayer she is also entitled to a £1,000 savings nil rate band, so the final £500 of her interest income is also tax free.

The first £5,000 of her dividend income is covered by the dividend nil rate band, the remaining £15,000 is taxed at 7.5%.

Example

Ollie is a company owner with a salary of £11,500 and dividends of £33,500. He also has interest income of £5,500 (total income £50,500).

There is no income tax on his salary and £5,000 of his interest income is tax free thanks to the 0% starting rate band (dividends do not count as non-savings income and do not use up the starting rate band).

Because his total income is £50,500 he is a higher-rate taxpayer and is entitled to a £500 savings nil rate band, so the final £500 of his interest income will also be tax free.

Turning to his dividend income, Ollie has £28,000 of his basic-rate band remaining (£45,000 - £11,500 - £5,500). Of this £5,000 will be tax free thanks to the dividend nil rate band and £23,000 will be taxed at 7.5%. The final £5,500 of his dividend income is taxed at 32.5%.

Although all of Ollie's interest is tax free it uses up some of his basic-rate band, pushing an equivalent amount of his dividend income over the higher-rate threshold where it is taxed at 32.5%.

Example

Mark is a company owner with a salary and rental income totalling £50,000 (his non-savings income) and dividend income of £20,000. He also has interest income of £5,000. His total income is £75,000.

Because his taxable non-savings income exceeds the £5,000 starting rate limit, none of his interest income is covered by the 0% starting rate. Furthermore, because he is a higher-rate taxpayer he is entitled to a £500 savings nil rate band. The final £4,500 of his interest income is taxed at 40%.

Turning to his dividend income, the first £5,000 will be tax free thanks to the dividend nil rate band and the final £15,000 is taxed at 32.5%.

Scottish Company Owners with Interest Income

The Scottish Parliament can now set its own income tax rates and thresholds for most types of income but dividends and interest income are taxed using UK rates and thresholds.

In other words, Scottish taxpayers will not pay more tax on their interest and dividend income than taxpayers living in other parts of the UK.

For the current 2017/18 tax year a Scottish company owner will only face a higher income tax bill if their other income (e.g. salary and rental income) is more than £43,000 – the Scottish higher-rate threshold.

Thus all of the previous examples are equally relevant to Scottish company owners. The only difference is Mark in the above example will pay £400 more tax on his salary and rental income.

Stock Market Dividends

The big difference between dividends from your own company and stock market companies is that stock market dividends can be completely sheltered from income tax in an ISA or SIPP.

In practice, many investors do in fact end up with a mixture of shares held inside and outside the tax protection of ISAs and SIPPs (for example, those who inherit a big share portfolio or want to invest more than the current £20,000 ISA limit but do not want to put money in a pension).

These investors could consider:

- Holding high-income shares inside an ISA (to protect the dividends from income tax), and

- Holding growth shares that produce capital gains outside an ISA (because up to £11,300 of capital gains will be tax free anyway thanks to the annual CGT exemption).

This simplistic strategy will not always produce the biggest tax savings, however. If you bought Apple shares back in 2003 – before their 12,000% rise – you would be kicking yourself if you didn't stick them in an ISA!

Stock Market Dividends – How Big a Problem?

Unlike dividends from your own company, you cannot control the amount of income you receive from stock market companies.

So if you have significant dividends from stock market companies, and the shares are not sheltered inside an ISA or SIPP, you may want to reduce the dividends you extract from your own company to avoid going over one of the key income tax thresholds.

However, my gut feeling is that stock market dividends do not cause tax problems for most individuals. The main exception is wealthy investors who hold a significant portfolio of shares outside a tax wrapper.

Even if you own, say, £100,000 worth of shares outside an ISA or SIPP you will probably receive no more than £3,500 per year in dividends, producing an income tax bill of £1,138 for a higher-rate taxpayer.

Short-term (Emergency) Tax Planning

If your total taxable income is higher than expected, there are some steps you can take to reduce it before the end of the tax year:

Pension Contributions

Everyone under age 75 can make a gross pension contribution of £3,600 per year. The taxpayer personally contributes £2,880 and the taxman tops up the pension plan with £720 of basic-rate tax relief. To make bigger pension contributions you require earnings: generally salary income or self-employment profits.

If you have a salary of £8,164 you can make a gross pension contribution of £8,164 (£6,531 from you, £1,633 from the taxman). Your basic-rate band will be increased by £8,164 so £8,164 of your dividends may escape higher-rate tax.

If you have self-employment income you can generally make an additional gross pension contribution equivalent to the taxable profits of the business, thereby eliminating any tax problem caused by this type of income.

See Chapters 24 and 25 for more on pension contributions.

Tax Deductible Expenditure

Self-employed business owners (sole traders and partnerships) can also reduce their taxable income by incurring tax deductible expenditure before the end of the business's tax year.

Possibly the easiest way is to incur expenditure that qualifies for an immediate tax deduction thanks to the annual investment allowance.

The allowance has now been fixed permanently at £200,000.

Property investors with higher than expected rental profits can spend money on property repairs before the end of the tax year, e.g. replacement kitchens and bathrooms.

Long-term Tax Planning

Company owners with significant amounts of income from other sources may be able to take the following steps to shift income from themselves to another entity or person:

Self-Employment Income

Consider putting the business into a second company (company 2) so that corporation tax is payable rather than income tax.

Dividends can then be extracted from company 2, taking into account dividends withdrawn from company 1. This will allow you to control your income tax bill from year to year.

Of course, it's not always advantageous to incorporate a second business. Sole traders and partnerships enjoy certain tax benefits, including more generous tax treatment of various expenses (including home office, travel and car capital allowances).

Rental Income

- Transferring properties to your spouse if he/she pays income tax at a lower rate.

- Holding commercial properties inside a pension scheme.

- Holding investment properties inside a company, so that corporation tax is payable instead of income tax and the extraction of rental profits (as dividends) can be controlled. See the Taxcafe guide *Using a Property Company to Save Tax* for a full discussion of the benefits and drawbacks of using a company.

- Consider alternative investments (e.g. blue chip shares) that can be sheltered from tax in an ISA or pension scheme.

Interest Income

Some company owners can receive up to £6,000 of tax-free interest and most can receive at least £500 (except additional-rate taxpayers). Where tax is payable on your interest income, or you fear it will push some of your dividend income into the 32.5% tax bracket, the following strategies can be adopted:

- Transfer savings into an ISA or SIPP.

- Use savings to pay off debt or take out an offset mortgage.

- Transfer cash to certain family members who pay tax at a lower rate.

- Invest in assets that produce capital growth rather than interest income.

Stock Market Dividends

- Hold shares in an ISA or SIPP.

- Transfer holdings to a spouse and possibly other family members.

Part 5

Splitting Income with Your Family

Chapter 20

Splitting Income with Your Spouse or Partner

In Chapter 11 we saw that couples can double up the tax-free salary and dividend and the amount of dividend income taxed at just 7.5%.

That's all very well if the couple own and run the company together. But what if your spouse/partner isn't involved in the business, for example if the company was started before you met or if they have a separate career and receive salary income from another employer?

In situations like these it may be possible to save income tax by gifting shares in the company to your spouse. It may even be possible to save tax by paying them a salary as well.

The amount of tax that can be saved depends on individual circumstances, for example how much profit the company makes and how much taxable income each person has already.

Tax savings are typically achieved where one spouse is a higher-rate taxpayer (paying 32.5% tax on their dividend income) and the other spouse has no income at all or is a basic-rate taxpayer.

However, it's not just these couples who can save tax. It's possible to pay income tax at more than 32.5% on dividend income that falls into any of the following tax brackets:

- £50,000-£60,000   Child benefit charge
- £100,000-£123,000   Personal allowance withdrawal
- Over £150,000   Additional-rate tax

If your income falls into one of these tax brackets you may be able to save tax by transferring income to your spouse, even if your spouse is a higher-rate taxpayer.

And because *every* taxpayer is entitled to a dividend allowance, it may be possible to save tax by shifting some dividend income to your spouse/partner, even if they're in the same tax bracket as you or a higher tax bracket. Unfortunately, the potential tax savings will be relatively modest in future because the dividend allowance is being reduced from £5,000 to £2,000 in April 2018.

Before we look at some sample tax savings it is important to point out that there are also potential dangers when it comes to splitting dividend income with your spouse. We will return to this important issue later in the chapter.

Capital Gains Tax

If you wish to split your dividend income with your spouse you generally have to transfer shares in the company to them.

In the case of married couples, a gift of shares would be exempt from capital gains tax.

Gifts between unmarried couples are normally subject to capital gains tax. However, the couple may be able to jointly elect to claim holdover relief.

Holdover relief allows a chargeable gain to be deferred (held over) when gifts of qualifying business assets are made. The person who receives the shares may eventually have to pay capital gains tax on your gain as well as their own when the shares are sold.

To qualify for holdover relief the company must generally be a regular trading company.

Unmarried couples who want to split their income face a further potential danger (see below).

Giving the Business Away

To successfully split your dividend income with your spouse it is essential that proper ownership of shares in the company is handed over. This means your spouse must be able to do what they like with any dividends paid out and with any capital growth from any sale of the business.

As we shall see shortly, it is also safer to transfer ordinary shares rather than shares that have fewer voting rights or other rights.

It is probably advisable to have any dividends received by your spouse paid into a separate bank account in their name, to illustrate to HMRC that you have not retained control of the money.

Dividends are generally payable in proportion to shareholdings. So if you normally take a dividend of £100,000 and want to transfer £40,000 of this income to your spouse, you will generally have to transfer 40% of the business to them.

Because this sort of tax planning, if done correctly, involves effectively giving away ownership and control of part of your business, it is only suitable where there is a significant amount of trust between the parties involved.

How Much of the Business Should Be Transferred?

For many company owners, a 50:50 ownership split with their spouse or partner will prove optimal, but a smaller stake can be transferred if the founder wants to retain more control over the business.

Example

Steve owns 100% of Steve's Spices, a small trading company. Steve currently pays himself a salary of £15,000 and dividends of £80,000.

His total income is £95,000 which means he is close to the £100,000 threshold. If his income rises above this threshold he will start to lose his income tax personal allowance.

As things stand he will pay income tax of £18,125 on his dividend income in 2017/18 – see Chapter 3 for an explanation of how dividends are taxed.

Steve's wife Lara does not own any shares in the company but she does receive rental income of £13,000 from a buy-to-let property.

This means she can receive dividends of up to £32,000 this year before she becomes a higher-rate taxpayer (£45,000 – £13,000). Of this, £5,000 will be tax-free this year and the rest will be taxed at just 7.5%.

Steve therefore transfers 40% of the ordinary shares in the business to Lara. The company continues to pay total dividends of £80,000 but now Steve's dividend is £48,000 and Lara's is £32,000.

Lara's total taxable income is now £45,000 and the tax bill on her dividend income is £2,025. Steve's total taxable income is now £63,000 and the tax bill on his dividend income is £7,725.

The tax on the total dividend income has been reduced by £8,375.

Furthermore, Steve's income is now well below the £100,000 threshold which means he doesn't have to worry about losing his income tax personal allowance for now.

Additional tax savings may be achieved if the couple are currently receiving child benefit. As we know from Chapter 14, the maximum child benefit charge is payable if, like Steve, the highest earner in the household has income of more than £60,000.

But if Steve transfers 50% of the business to Lara, instead of 40%, his total taxable income will fall to £55,000.

Like Steve, Lara will pay 32.5% tax on the additional £8,000 of dividend income she will receive. However, because Steve's income is now £55,000 the child benefit charge will be reduced by 50%, saving the couple an additional £894 in 2017/18 if they have two children, with similar savings in future years (see Chapter 14).

Furthermore, some of Lara's additional £8,000 of dividend income will be taxed at 7.5% instead of 32.5% if the higher-rate threshold is gradually increased to at least £50,000 by 2020.

Potential Tax Savings

The potential tax savings from transferring dividend income to your spouse will vary from case to case:

Spouse Has No Taxable Income

If you are a basic-rate taxpayer (income under £45,000 in 2017/18) and your spouse is a 'house-spouse' with no taxable income, they can receive tax-free dividends of up to £16,500 in 2017/18 (made up of the £11,500 personal allowance and £5,000 dividend allowance). The potential tax saving is £1,238 (£16,500 x 7.5%).

If you are a higher-rate taxpayer and your spouse has no taxable income, they can receive less heavily taxed dividends of up to £45,000 in 2017/18. The first £16,500 will be tax free and £2,138 tax will be payable on the remaining £28,500 (at 7.5%).

Because you would pay £14,625 tax on the same income (£45,000 x 32.5%) the potential tax saving is £12,487 (£14,625 - £2,138).

The tax saving will be even greater if your income would otherwise exceed the £100,000 threshold where your personal allowance would be withdrawn.

Spouse is a Basic-Rate Taxpayer

Even if your spouse works and has taxable income, it may be possible to save tax by gifting shares in the business to them. Again, the tax savings will vary from case to case.

Example
Rupert is a company owner who expects to have a taxable income of £60,000 in 2017/18, made up of a £50,000 dividend and £10,000 of salary and other income. He will pay 32.5% tax on £15,000 of his dividend income (£60,000 - £45,000 higher-rate threshold).

His wife, Wendy, receives taxable income of £30,000 from another source. Thus she has £15,000 of her basic-rate band left and can receive up to £15,000 of dividend income that will be less heavily taxed in her hands.

If Rupert gifts 25% of the shares to Wendy and the company normally pays dividends of £50,000, she'll receive £12,500. The first £5,000 will currently be tax free thanks to the dividend allowance and tax of £563 will be payable on the remaining £7,500 (at 7.5%). Rupert would've paid £4,063 tax on this income (at 32.5%) so the tax saving is £3,500.

Spouse is a Higher-Rate Taxpayer

If you and your spouse/partner are both higher-rate taxpayers (income over £45,000 in 2017/18) it may still possible to save tax by gifting them shares in the company. Not only does your spouse have their own dividend allowance but evening up your income may help you avoid the child benefit charge.

Example revisited
The facts are exactly the same as before except Wendy's income is £45,000 instead of £30,000 and she receives £1,789 child benefit for two children. As things stand, the couple's child benefit will be completely withdrawn because Rupert's income is £60,000.

If Rupert gifts 15% of the business to Wendy she will receive dividends of £7,500 and his income will fall to £52,500. She will pay no tax on the first £5,000 this year, whereas Rupert would have paid 32.5%, so the saving is £1,625.

She will pay 32.5% tax on the other £2,500. However, her total taxable income is now £52,500, the same as Rupert's. By equalising their incomes in this fashion the couple will be able to hold onto three-quarters of their child benefit – a saving of £1,342 this year.

Transferable Tax Allowance for Married Couples

Married couples can transfer 10% of their personal allowances to each other (£1,150 during the current 2017/18 tax year). Only basic-rate taxpayers can benefit, so the potential tax saving is £230 (£1,150 x 20%).

Married couples can generally only benefit if one person earns less than £11,500 (i.e. is wasting some of their personal allowance). However, company owners with small dividends have more scope to benefit from this tax break:

Example
David owns a small company. In 2017/18 he takes a tax-free salary of £8,164 and dividends of £25,000, i.e. he's a basic-rate taxpayer. His wife Michelle doesn't own any shares in the company. She's a teacher with a salary of £30,000, i.e. also a basic-rate taxpayer.

If David elects to transfer £1,150 of his personal allowance to Michelle, this will save her £230 income tax on her salary. David will pay 7.5% tax on an additional £1,150 of dividend income: £86. So the overall net saving for the couple is £144.

This strategy won't work if David takes a salary of £11,500 instead. Although Michelle will save tax, David will pay £230 income tax on his own salary. It also won't work if David takes a salary of £8,164 and dividend of more than £35,686 in 2017/18 – reducing his personal allowance will push some of his dividend income into the higher-rate bracket – higher-rate taxpayers cannot transfer their personal allowances.

Why the Tax Savings May Not Last

There are many reasons why any tax savings that may be achieved in one tax year by splitting income with your spouse may not be achievable in full in future tax years, including:

- Changes to tax rates and thresholds
- Changes to personal circumstances

Changes to Tax Rates & Thresholds

It has been announced that the dividend allowance will be cut from £5,000 to £2,000 in April 2018. This will reduce the tax savings that may be achieved by shifting dividend income to a spouse who is in the same tax bracket as you, for example where you are both higher-rate taxpayers.

If the additional rate (income over £150,000) is eventually abolished this will eliminate most of the tax savings that can currently be achieved by shifting dividend income to a spouse who is a higher-rate taxpayer.

Further changes that eliminate tax savings cannot be ruled out.

Changes to Personal Circumstances

Because every taxpayer can benefit from the dividend allowance (£5,000 this year, £2,000 next year) it is possible to save some tax by shifting income to your spouse, even if your spouse pays tax at a higher rate than you.

Beyond the dividend allowance, income tax savings can generally only be achieved if your spouse has a lower tax rate than you.

It is possible that, over time, your tax rate will fall or your spouse's tax rate will increase. This could eliminate or even reverse any initial income tax saving that is achieved.

Your tax rate could fall if the company's profits fall, resulting in lower dividends. Your spouse's tax rate could rise if their income from other sources increases (for example, if another business they own produces bigger profits).

There are lots of different permutations. The key point is that couples should look further ahead than just one tax year when deciding what proportion of the company each should own.

HMRC's Attacks on Income Shifting

Income splitting arrangements like those described in this chapter have come under attack in recent years. In particular, the taxman has tried to prevent dividends being paid to non-working spouses or spouses who do just a small amount of work for the company.

In particular, the taxman's target has been small 'personal service' companies (IT consultants and the like) where most of the work is carried out by one person.

It all came to a head in the notorious 'Arctic Systems' tax case. HMRC tried to use the so-called settlements legislation to prevent Geoff Jones, a computer consultant, from splitting his dividend income with his wife.

The settlements legislation is designed to prevent income being shifted from one individual to another via a 'settlement', for example by transferring an asset or making some other 'arrangement'.

In the Arctic Systems case Mr Jones did most of the work in the company. Mrs Jones did a few hours admin each week. Because Mr Jones only paid himself a small salary despite all the work he did, more money was left to pay out as dividends to Mrs Jones. HMRC therefore decided that a settlement had taken place and tried to have Mrs Jones' dividend income taxed in her husband's hands.

HMRC originally won the case but the decision was overturned by the House of Lords.

The judges agreed with HMRC that a settlement had taken place **but** decided that the settlement provisions could not be applied because in this case the couple were protected by the exemption for gifts between spouses. This exemption applies where:

- There is an outright gift of property to a spouse, and
- The property is not wholly or mainly a right to income

On the first point, the judges ruled that, although Mrs Jones had subscribed for her share when the company was set up (i.e., it was not strictly speaking gifted to her by her husband), her share was essentially a gift because it contained an 'element of bounty': the share provided a benefit that Mr Jones would not have given to a complete stranger.

On the second point, the judges also ruled that a gift of *ordinary* shares is not wholly or mainly a right to income because ordinary shares have other rights: voting rights and the right to capital gains if the company is sold.

Thanks to the courage of Mr and Mrs Jones, who were prepared to fight HMRC all the way to the House of Lords, this exemption should safeguard most types of income splitting arrangements between married couples where ordinary shares are involved.

For this reason many tax advisers are of the opinion that married couples should make hay while the sun shines, i.e. they should split their dividend income with their spouses while they can.

Preference Shares

The outcome of the Arctic Systems case may have been different if another type of share other than ordinary shares had been involved.

In another tax case (*Young v Pearce*), wives were issued with preference shares that paid income but had very few other rights. The shares did not have voting rights and did not entitle the spouses to receive any payout in the event of the company being sold (other than the original £25 payment for the shares).

All that the preference shares provided was a right to receive 30% of the company's profits as a dividend. The court therefore decided that the preference shares provided wholly or mainly a right to income.

Thus the exemption for gifts between spouses was not available and the settlement rules applied. The wives' dividends were therefore taxed in the hands of their husbands.

Unmarried Couples & Other Family Members

Although HMRC was defeated in the Arctic Systems case, the judges did agree that a settlement had taken place. The taxpayers only won the case thanks to the exemption for gifts between *spouses*.

There is still uncertainty as to where this leaves income-splitting arrangements between other groups of individuals, in particular, *unmarried* couples.

HMRC probably does take the view that the settlements legislation applies to unmarried couples and other family members, especially where small personal service companies are involved.

However, to date the taxman has not pursued these individuals aggressively so, again, it may be a case of making hay while the sun shines.

To protect against any potential attack the best defence is probably to have both individuals equally involved in the business (a bit of admin or bookkeeping will not suffice, as Mr and Mrs Jones discovered.)

HMRC's main concern seems to be personal service companies (IT consultants and other businesses where the profits are generated from one person's services). Larger businesses that have other employees, premises, equipment etc may be safer because the profits come from various sources, not just one person's work.

Danger Ahead?

In 2007 draft income shifting legislation was published but fortunately never made it onto the statute books after being widely condemned for being completely unworkable.

That draft legislation essentially sought to prevent business owners from receiving dividends unless they effectively earned them! This would have undermined the whole basis of shareholder capitalism – dividends are supposed to be a reward for being an entrepreneur and setting up or investing in a business.

Although income shifting legislation is on the back burner for now, it could be introduced in the future and could upset some income splitting arrangements.

Dividend Waivers

Dividend waivers are used by company owners who wish to relinquish their rights to dividends. They can be commercially justifiable, for example if a shareholder waives his dividend to protect the company's cash.

To be effective it is necessary to draw up a formal deed which is executed before the dividend is declared or paid.

Company owners have also tried to use dividend waivers to avoid tax by diverting income to their spouses. For example, a higher-rate taxpayer may try to divert a disproportionate share of the company's profit to his spouse who is a basic-rate taxpayer.

HMRC may use the settlements legislation to attack arrangements where shareholders end up with excessive dividends, i.e. more of the company's distributable profit than their shareholding would normally entitle them to. Because dividend waivers involve simply a transfer of income, not assets, they are not protected by the exemption for outright gifts to spouses (see above).

Example

Mrs M owns 80 ordinary shares in M Limited and also has a significant amount of taxable income from other sources. Mr M owns 20 shares and has no other income. The company has retained profits of £50,000. Mrs M waives her right to a dividend and the company then declares a dividend of £2,000 per share. Mr M thus receives a dividend of £40,000, most of which he hopes will be taxed at no more than 7.5%.

HMRC could apply the settlements legislation in this situation. Clearly a dividend of £2,000 per share could not have been paid on all 100 shares, so the waiver enhanced Mr M's dividend.

This would therefore be seen as a "bounteous arrangement" – it is unlikely Mrs M would have agreed to do the same thing with a third party. £32,000 of the dividend paid to Mr M would therefore be taxed in Mrs M's hands.

Some of the things HMRC will look for when deciding whether to apply the settlements legislation to dividend waivers include:

- Insufficient retained profits to pay the same rate of dividend on all issued share capital.

- Even if there is sufficient profit to pay the same rate of dividend per share for the year in question, there has been a succession of waivers over several years and, in the absence of the waivers, the total dividends payable exceed the company's retained profits.

- Waiving shareholders wish to benefit non-waiving shareholders.

- Non-waiving shareholders pay tax at a lower rate.

In summary, company owners should be careful of entering into arrangements to waive dividends where there is no commercial reason for the waivers and no evidence that the waivers are for non-tax reasons.

Salaries for Spouses

If your partner also works for your company they can be paid a salary. Please note, you cannot pay them a salary if they do no work for the company. And you cannot pay them more than the market rate. If you do, the company will be denied tax relief for the expense.

If your partner has no taxable income from other sources, a small salary will be more tax efficient than simply paying them dividends.

Why? Unlike dividends which are paid out of the company's after-tax profits, salaries are a tax deductible expense for the company. In other words, in addition to any *income tax* savings enjoyed by the couple, a salary will also save the company *corporation tax*.

For example, a small salary of £8,164 will save a company £1,551 in corporation tax (at 19%).

To avoid national insurance, salary payments should be made monthly instead of as a lump sum. If, however, your spouse is a director the payment can be made as a lump sum because company directors pay national insurance on an annual basis.

Second Jobs

What if your spouse already has income from other sources, e.g. a salary from another job? Is it still tax efficient to get your company to pay them a small salary?

Firstly, it's important to point out that, if your spouse works for another employer, the employment contract may prevent them working for you as well.

If there is no such restriction, paying your spouse a small salary could lead to an overall saving of several hundred pounds in some cases. Why? Because for basic-rate taxpayers the combined tax rate (corporation tax and income tax) for dividend income is now roughly 25%, compared with 20% for salaries.

Thus paying your spouse a salary of, say, £8,164 could lead to an overall saving of just over £400 (£8,164 x 5%), providing there is no national insurance payable.

The savings may be much smaller or non-existent in other cases, for example for some higher-rate taxpayers, so it may be necessary to do some calculations specific to your circumstances.

Chapter 21

Splitting Income with Your Children

Dividends

It is possible to gift shares in your company to your children. Because they will have their own income tax personal allowance and dividend nil-rate band it may be possible for them to receive tax-free dividends of up to £16,500 each in 2017/18, plus an additional £28,500 taxed at just 7.5%.

However, it is important to point out that this type of tax planning generally only works when *adult* children are involved (i.e. children 18 or older).

Transfers of income to minor children are generally ineffective and the income would be taxed in the parent's hands.

This section therefore deals exclusively with adult children.

If you gift shares in the company to your adult children there will potentially be capital gains tax payable, as if you had sold the shares to them for their full market value. However, it may be possible for both the parent and child to jointly elect to hold over the capital gain.

To qualify for holdover relief the company must, generally speaking, be a trading company.

The safest route is probably to use ordinary shares, which means your children will obtain full ownership and voting rights in respect of their share of the business, not just a right to receive dividends.

There is a potential tax trap for family members who are gifted shares and are also employees of the company. In certain cases, where shares are obtained because of an individual's employment, a gift of shares can be subject to employment income tax charges.

However, there is an exemption where shares are given in the 'normal course of domestic, family or personal relationships'. So in most family companies, where shares are transferred to a spouse or adult children, the transfer should not give rise to any employment tax charges.

There is nevertheless a danger that, in certain circumstances, HMRC may argue that the individuals received shares by virtue of their employment, not because they are family members.

For example, if the individual only receives a small salary from the company (i.e. below market rate) HMRC may have more grounds to argue that the gift was made to increase the individual's remuneration from the company.

If shares are transferred to a family member who is an employee and to other employees who are not family members, this could indicate that the gift was made because of the family member's employment.

On the other hand, if shares are gifted to several family members (some of whom are not employees) this may indicate that the gift was made solely because of the family relationship.

It may be wise in such circumstances to document the reasons for the gift and (as always) obtain professional advice.

Salaries for Children

It's often worth getting your company to employ your children (including your minor children) at certain points in time. The salary payments will generally be a tax deductible expense for the business, providing the payments can be justified by the duties performed.

Furthermore, the income will generally be tax free in the hands of the children, if they're at school or university and have no other taxable income.

A tax deduction coupled with a tax-free receipt is the best possible outcome when it comes to extracting money from your company!

Those aged under 16 can be paid up to £11,500 in 2017/18 with no income tax or national insurance consequences.

Children who are 16 and over have to pay 12% employee's national insurance on income over £8,164.

However, employers do not have to pay national insurance on salaries paid to under 21s as long as their earnings do not exceed the higher-rate threshold (currently £45,000). This exemption also extends to apprentices who are under 25.

It is important to take note of the restrictions placed on the hours and types of work that children can do because this will affect how much you can pay them.

Restrictions on Work and Hours

Children are of compulsory school age up to the last Friday in June in the academic year of their 16th birthday. After this they are at the 'mandatory school leaving age' and can apply for a national insurance number and work full time.

Until that time there are restrictions on the hours and types of work that can be carried out. For starters, it is generally illegal to employ children under 13 in any capacity (unless they're involved in TV and modelling).

Other children must not work:

- Without an employment permit if local byelaws require it
- In factories or on industrial sites
- During school hours
- Before 7.00 am or after 7.00 pm
- For more than 1 hour before school (local byelaws permitting)
- For more than 4 hours without taking a 1 hour break
- In occupations prohibited by byelaws/legislation (e.g. pubs)
- If the work will harm their health, well-being or education
- Without having a 2 week break during the school holidays in each calendar year

More Restrictions on Hours Worked

During term time children can work for no more than 12 hours per week including a maximum of:

- 2 hours on school days and Sundays
- 5 hours on Saturdays for 13 to 14 year olds; 8 hours for 15 to 16 year olds

During school holidays 13 to 14 year olds may work a maximum of 25 hours per week. This includes a maximum of:

- 5 hours on weekdays and Saturdays
- 2 hours on Sunday

During school holidays 15 to 16 year olds may work a maximum of 35 hours per week. This includes a maximum of:

- 8 hours on weekdays and Saturdays
- 2 hours on Sunday

National Minimum Wage & Living Wage

If your children are below the compulsory school leaving age the national minimum wage does not apply. The hourly rates for older children are currently as follows:

- £7.50   Living wage, 25 and over
- £7.05   21-24
- £5.60   18-20
- £4.05   16-17 if above school leaving age
- £3.50   apprentice rate

Part 6

Other Profit Extraction Strategies

Chapter 22

Loans to Directors

It used to be illegal for companies to make loans to directors. This is no longer the case. Since October 2007, loans of any size have been permitted.

With the exception of loans for under £10,000 they do generally have to be approved by the company's shareholders.

Obviously, for most small companies, this is not a problem because the shareholders and directors are the same people!

You cannot take a loan from your company for an indefinite period without any tax consequences. If that were possible most company owners would never pay themselves taxable dividends.

The attractiveness of taking a loan from your company is limited by two potential tax charges:

- a 32.5% company tax charge (section 455 charge)
- a benefit-in-kind charge

The section 455 tax charge was recently increased from 25% to 32.5% and applies to loans made on or after 6 April 2016.

Fortunately, it is possible to avoid or mitigate the damage caused by these taxes, if you understand the rules.

The Section 455 Charge

Most private companies are 'close companies'. If you are a director/shareholder of a close company you are known as a 'participator'. Some other shareholders are also classed as participators.

If a company lends money to a participator *the company* will have to pay a 32.5% tax charge on the loan. This is known as the section 455 charge (previously known as the section 419 charge). Failure to pay this charge will result in penalties and interest.

However, there are two reasons why this charge is not as bad as it first appears:

#1 Short-term Loans Escape the Section 455 Charge

The 32.5% tax does not apply if the loan is repaid within nine months of the company's financial year end. This is the normal due date for the company's corporation tax. This means that short-term loans to directors do not attract a tax charge.

Example
Bill Ltd's financial year ends on 31 December 2017. The company made a £10,000 loan to Bill, the sole shareholder and director, in January 2017.

Bill repays the loan before the end of September 2018. The company will not have to pay the 32.5% tax charge because the loan was repaid within 9 months of the end of the accounting period in which it was made.

Example
The facts are the same as before except only £7,000 is repaid before the end of September 2018. The remaining £3,000 is repaid in October 2019. The company will pay a section 455 tax charge of £975 (£3,000 x 32.5%).

#2 The Section 455 Charge is Refundable

Even if the 32.5% tax does end up being paid because the loan is not repaid early enough, the tax will be refunded when the loan is repaid.

That's the good news. The bad news is the company will only be repaid 9 months after the end of the accounting period in which the loan is repaid.

In Bill Ltd's case this means the £975 tax will be repaid on 1 October 2020.

Exemption for Minority Shareholders

This exemption isn't much use to most small company owners. Nevertheless it is worth mentioning that there is no 32.5% company tax charge if you own 5% or less of the company's ordinary shares.

There are a number of qualifying criteria:

- Total loans to the individual cannot exceed £15,000
- The individual must work full time in the business

When it comes to the 5% limit you must include shares owned by you, your spouse and other 'associates' (e.g. close relatives).

Although there is no company tax charge on small loans to minority shareholders, there will still be a potential benefit-in-kind charge.

Benefit-in-kind Charge

If no interest is payable on the loan or if the interest paid is less than the 'official rate', the director will have to pay an income tax benefit-in-kind charge.

The official rate of interest is currently 3%, so if the interest charged on the loan is less than 3%, a benefit-in-kind charge is payable.

For example, if the loan is for £20,000 and no interest is charged, the director will face the following benefit-in-kind charge if he is a higher-rate taxpayer:

£20,000 loan x 3% interest x 40% tax = £240

The company will also have to pay class 1A national insurance:

£20,000 loan x 3% interest x 13.8% = £82.80

The benefit in kind is reduced if interest is paid to the company. For example, if you pay 1% interest, the benefit in kind will be calculated using an interest rate of 2% (3% less 1%).

Note, however, that the benefit in kind is only reduced if there is a formal obligation to pay interest to the company. For this reason it is probably advisable to have a properly drawn up loan agreement.

If you do pay interest on the loan, the good news is that you will be paying the money to your own company rather than a bank. However, the company will pay corporation tax on the interest it receives.

It must also be remembered that money inside a company is generally less valuable than money outside a company. If you wish to withdraw the interest back out as a dividend, there is likely to be an income tax charge.

Should Directors Pay Interest?

Let's compare two scenarios:

- An interest-free loan
- Paying interest at the official rate

We will assume that the loan is for £20,000, the official interest rate is 3% and the director is a 40% taxpayer.

#1 Interest-free loan

The benefit-in-kind charge paid by the director will be:

$$£20,000 \times 3\% \times 40\% = £240$$

The national insurance paid by the company will be:

$$£20,000 \times 3\% \times 13.8\% = £83$$

The employer's national insurance is itself a tax deductible expense, so the net cost would actually be £67 (£83 less 19% corporation tax relief).

$$\text{Total cost of loan: } £240 + £67 = £307$$

#2 Interest at the official rate

On a £20,000 loan the director will pay £600 interest to the company (£20,000 x 3%). The company will then pay corporation tax on this interest, so the cost is £114:

$$£600 \times 19\% \text{ corporation tax} = £114$$

Even if the after-tax interest is taken back out as a dividend, producing an income tax charge of £158 for a higher-rate taxpayer (£486 x 32.5%), the total tax cost will be less than for an interest-free loan.

In summary, it is generally cheaper, at present, to pay interest at the official rate, rather than take an interest-free loan.

The Official Rate of Interest

Back in 2009 the official rate of interest was 6.25%. If and when interest rates are eventually increased, the official rate of interest will also be increased and this will affect the cost of directors' loans.

The current and previous official rates can be found here:

www.hmrc.gov.uk/rates/interest-beneficial.htm

Exemptions from the Benefit in Kind Charge

There are two important exemptions from benefit in kind charges:

- Loans to invest in another company
- Loans for less than £10,000

Note that neither of these two exemptions make any difference to the requirement to pay the section 455 company tax charge.

Remember, however, that the company tax charge does not apply to short-term loans (up to 21 months) and is repayable.

Benefit-in-kind exemption #1
Loans to invest in another company

There is generally no benefit in kind charge on certain *qualifying* loans. A qualifying loan is one where the interest (if interest was charged) would be tax deductible.

An example of a qualifying loan would be one given to an individual so that he can acquire an interest in another close trading company.

The person borrowing the money must generally hold more than 5% of the ordinary shares in the company in which the money is being invested.

Whether this is the most tax-efficient way to finance a new business venture is, of course, another question altogether.

Remember that the section 455 company tax charge still applies, unless the loan is repaid within 9 months of the end of the accounting period in which it is made.

Benefit-in-kind exemption #2
Loans under £10,000

There is no benefit-in-kind charge if all of the loans to the director/shareholder total £10,000 or less throughout the tax year.

It is important to understand that any sum due from the director to the company is counted as a 'loan', including goods or services that have been provided to the director but not paid for.

The section 455 corporation tax charge still applies if the loan is not repaid on time. Nevertheless, this exemption currently allows a director/shareholder to take a loan of up to £10,000 for up to 21 months with no adverse tax consequences.

Even if you just take the money and stick it in a cash ISA, the exemption may provide an opportunity to save some tax and earn more interest. Company accounts often pay much less interest than the best deals on individual savings accounts.

Example

Let's say Jack and Jill, both directors of Jack and Jill Ltd, take loans of £10,000 each (£20,000 in total) at the beginning of the company's financial year. They stick the money in ISAs earning 1.5% tax free.

They repay the loans 21 months later, just in time to prevent the company paying the 32.5% section 455 tax charge. In total, they will have earned around £500 tax free, compared with the £35 or so of taxable interest the company would have earned.

Larger Short-term Loans

In the above example, by taking a loan for no more than £10,000 and repaying it on time, both the 32.5% section 455 tax charge and the benefit-in-kind charge were avoided.

What if you want to borrow more than the tax-free limit for a short period – how does this compare with paying yourself additional taxable dividends?

Example

Penelope owns Pitstop Hotels Ltd which has a 31 December accounting date. Penelope normally withdraws a small salary and enough dividend income to use up her basic-rate band.

It's the beginning of January 2018 and Penelope would like to withdraw an additional £20,000 from Pitstop Hotels, over and above her usual salary and dividends. She intends to use the money to pay for some home improvements.

If she takes the money as a dividend there will be an income tax charge of £6,500 payable by 31 January 2019.

Instead she decides to takes a loan of £20,000 from her company on 6 January 2018. Because the loan is for more than £10,000 she will be subject to a benefit-in-kind charge, unless she pays interest to her company at the official rate.

The loan will also be subject to the 32.5% section 455 tax charge unless it is repaid by the end of September 2019 (9 months after the end of the company's accounting period on 31 December 2018).

She decides to pay interest to her company at the official rate and to repay the loan on 5 September 2019, i.e. after 20 months. Assuming the official rate of interest is 3%, the total interest payable to Pitstop Hotels will be £1,000:

$$£20,000 \times 3\% \times 20/12 = £1,000$$

The corporation tax payable on the interest is £190 (£1,000 x 19%). This is effectively the cost of the loan.

To repay the loan Penelope withdraws additional dividend income, over and above what she normally takes, of £20,000 on 6 April 2019. The income tax on this additional dividend is £6,500, payable by 31 January 2021.

By taking a loan in 2018 instead of a taxable dividend, Penelope has managed to defer paying income tax of £6,500 for two years. The total cost is just £190.

Additional points to note:

- If Penelope's marginal income tax rate in 2019/20 is significantly higher than in 2017/18 then she may be better off paying herself a dividend in January 2018 instead of taking a loan. In particular she may have to watch out for the £50,000, £100,000 and £150,000 thresholds.

- If Penelope can repay the loan out of her regular dividend income taxed at just 7.5% (i.e. without having to withdraw an additional dividend taxed at 32.5%) she may be able to *save* £6,500 in income tax, not just defer paying it.

Loans to Directors – Other Issues

Loans to Family

You cannot necessarily avoid the section 455 tax charge and benefit-in-kind charge by making loans to family members.

For example, both the section 455 charge and the benefit-in-kind charge apply to loans to spouses and children of the director/shareholder and other close relatives. The section 455 charge also applies to loans to business partners.

The charges do not apply to loans to friends and some more distant relatives BUT you will incur the taxman's wrath if the benefit of the loan passes back to you or a close relative.

Loan Written Off

If the loan is formally released or written off by the company, the amount is likely to be treated as a deemed dividend for income tax purposes.

However, in most instances the amount released will also be subject to national insurance payable by both the employee and employer.

Because of this national insurance cost you may wish to consider declaring a dividend to settle the debt, providing the company has sufficient distributable reserves.

A loan written off in these circumstances will not be deductible for corporation tax purposes.

Any section 455 tax charge paid is, however, refunded to the company if the loan is released or written off.

The safest course of action may be to ensure that any loan is always repaid, wherever possible, rather than written off.

Paperwork

Although it's simple in small companies to obtain shareholder approval for loans, it's important to get the paperwork right.

There should be a proper loan agreement with written documentation outlining the nature of the loan, the company's liability and the amount and purpose of the loan.

The shareholders must then grant their approval at a meeting or by written resolution, again with all the appropriate documentation.

Shareholder approval is not required for loans of up to £10,000, although it is good practice to continue to produce the same paperwork, where possible, as this may provide more certainty as to the tax treatment of the borrowed money.

Financial Reporting Standard 102 (FRS 102)

A new financial reporting standard (FRS 102) may affect the accounting treatment of directors' loans in certain circumstances.

Where interest is not charged at a market rate the loan may have to be discounted in the company's accounts. For example, if the market interest rate is 5% and an interest-free loan of £100,000 is made to a director and is repayable after three years, the present value of the loan is £86,384:

$$£100,000/(1.05 \times 1.05 \times 1.05) = £86,384$$

The initial shortfall of £13,616 would be treated as a 'distribution'.

The tax treatment does not, however, follow the accounting treatment. The section 455 charge is still based on the total amount of the loan and the director's taxable benefit will be calculated in the way described earlier in this chapter.

To avoid the complexities of FRS 102, tax commentators suggest that it should be specifically recorded that directors' loan accounts are repayable on demand or to make sure that a market rate of interest is charged.

Loan Recycling

HMRC didn't like it when loans to directors were repaid before the section 455 charge was payable, with new loans taken out straight away (known as 'bed and breakfasting'). Thus a number of changes came into operation on 20 March 2013:

The 30 Day Rule

Relief from the section 455 tax is denied if:

- A shareholder makes repayments totalling £5,000 or more to the company and within 30 days...

- new loans totalling £5,000 or more are made to the same person or their associates

For this rule to apply, the original loan and repayment can take place in the same or different accounting periods. The new loan must be in a subsequent accounting period to the original loan.

It's important to point out that the 30-day rule does not apply where the loan is repaid using amounts that give rise to an income tax charge, for example where a taxable dividend is declared and credited to the director's loan account.

Example 1

During accounting period 1 there is a loan outstanding of £6,000. Two days before the end of the accounting period £6,000 is repaid. Three days into accounting period 2 a new £6,000 loan is taken. The repayment will be matched with the new loan, not the old loan. The loan from accounting period 1 is treated as still outstanding and will be subject to the section 455 tax charge if not repaid.

Example 2

C Ltd is a close company in which Jim is a shareholder. C Ltd's accounting period ends on 31 March 2018. On 25 March 2018, Jim borrows £15,000 from C Ltd. If the loan is not repaid within nine months of the end of the accounting period, C Ltd must pay a 32.5% section 455 tax charge (£4,875).

On 1 December 2018, a dividend of £9,000 is declared by C Ltd on which Jim is chargeable to income tax. On the same day, Jim repays the remaining £6,000. On 10 December 2018, Jim borrows £3,500 from the company. On 15 December 2018, Jim borrows a further £2,000 from the company.

The section 455 tax charge is calculated as follows:

- £9,000 was repaid by applying a chargeable dividend towards the loan. This is ignored when it comes to applying the 30 day rule. The remaining £6,000 that Jim repays exceeds the £5,000 minimum repayment under the 30-day rule.

- Nine days later and 14 days later respectively (i.e. within 30 days) Jim withdraws a further £5,500 (£3,500 + £2,000) which is also in excess of the £5,000 limit for new loans.

- The new loans (£5,500) are less than the repayments (£6,000). Relief from the section 455 tax charge is denied on the lesser amount of £5,500, resulting in a tax charge of £1,788. Only the real repayment of £500 is recognised.

The Arrangements Rule

This rule applies even if the new borrowing takes place after 30 days. Relief from the section 455 tax will be denied if:

- Prior to repaying the loan, the total amount owed by the shareholder to the company is £15,000 or more, and

- At the time of the repayment, arrangements had been made for new loans of £5,000 or more to replace the amounts repaid.

The relief denied is the lower of the amount repaid and the new loan.

'Arrangements' are not defined and HMRC will give the term a wide meaning.

Once again, the arrangements rule does not apply if the loan is repaid with a taxable dividend or bonus. In other words, if a loan account is credited with a taxable dividend this will be treated as a valid loan repayment.

Example

Brigitte owes her company Bard Ltd £25,000 which she borrowed on 1 June 2017 during the accounting period ending 30 June 2017.

After the end of the accounting period, Brigitte takes a 45-day loan from the bank for £25,000 and uses it to repay the loan to her company. 40 days after repaying her company, Brigitte takes a new loan of £30,000 from her company and uses it to repay the bank.

There is a significant risk that HMRC will argue that, at the time she repaid her company, Brigitte had made arrangements to withdraw a new amount from her company (to repay the bank loan), so the original loan will be treated as not repaid. As a result, the section 455 tax will become payable on the initial £25,000 loan, unless a further repayment is made.

What is a Valid Income Tax Charge?

As mentioned above, the anti-avoidance rules do not apply if the amount repaid gives rise to an income tax charge in the hands of the director-shareholder.

This will be the case if a loan is repaid by means of a dividend credited to the director's loan account which is included as income on the director's tax return (or where a bonus is paid which is subject to PAYE before being credited to the director's loan account).

According to HMRC, if a dividend is first paid out in cash and the money is then paid back into the company and credited to the director's loan account, the exemption does not apply.

HMRC also contends that, if the director owns the business premises and the company pays him rent, the exemption does not apply to rent credited to the director's loan account.

Chapter 23

Rental Income: Better than Dividends

Should you get your company to pay you rent?

Many company owners own their business premises *personally* and the company pays them rent.

Paying yourself rent is often more tax efficient than paying yourself a higher salary. Like salaries, rental payments are a tax deductible expense (providing the rent does not exceed the market rent). But, unlike salaries, there is no national insurance cost.

Following the recent increase in dividend tax rates, rental income is also more tax efficient than dividend income in many cases.

Of course, there are also non-tax reasons why you may wish to pay yourself rental income instead of withdrawing dividends from your company. For starters, to pay dividends the company must have sufficient distributable profits. There is no such requirement when it comes to paying rent.

Secondly, with rental income it is relatively straightforward to pay yourself a fixed monthly amount throughout the year, for example by setting up a direct debit from your company bank account to your personal bank account. This could be helpful if you have to personally pay various costs associated with the property, especially mortgage interest.

With rental income there is no requirement to continually do all the paperwork that often accompanies dividend payments, for example holding directors' board meetings and shareholder meetings.

How much better off could you be by paying yourself rental income instead of dividends? It all depends on your personal circumstances, for example how much taxable income you have and the amount of tax deductible mortgage interest you have.

Example – Basic-rate Taxpayer

Warren is a company owner and a basic-rate taxpayer. He personally owns the property out of which the company operates but the company currently doesn't pay him any rent. He does not have any tax deductible mortgage interest to offset.

During the current 2017/18 tax year he decides to pay himself a small tax-free salary of £8,164. He also has other taxable income which uses up the balance of his £11,500 income tax personal allowance. He withdraws the rest of the company's profits as dividends.

Let's say he gets the company to pay him rental income of £10,000 per year. After paying income tax at 20% he will be left with £8,000.

If the company had not paid him rent it would have had an extra £8,100 to pay out as dividends (£10,000 less 19% corporation tax). Warren would have been left with £7,493 after paying 7.5% income tax.

By getting the company to pay him rent Warren is better off by just over £500. For basic-rate taxpayers the combined tax rate on dividends is roughly 25%, compared with 20% for rental income.

Example 1 – Higher-rate Taxpayer

The facts are exactly the same except the company has bigger profits and so Warren has more dividend income and is a higher-rate taxpayer. If he gets the company to pay him rental income of £10,000, after paying income tax at 20% he will be left with £8,000.

However, his rental income will use up £10,000 of his basic-rate band which means £10,000 of his dividend income will be taxed at 32.5% instead of 7.5%, resulting in additional tax of £2,500. Overall Warren will be left with £5,500 (£8,000 - £2,500).

If the company had not paid him any rental income, it would have been left with an extra £8,100 to pay out as dividends and Warren would have been left with £5,467 after paying income tax at 32.5%.

Rental income is still more tax efficient than dividend income but in this example the saving is very small – just £33 on £10,000 of rental income!

In some other cases higher-rate taxpayers will save significantly more tax by paying themselves rental income:

Example 2 – Higher-rate Taxpayer

This time we'll assume that Warren's premises are more substantial and he gets the company to pay him rental income of £33,500. Along with his salary and other income this will take him up to the £45,000 higher-rate threshold. After paying 20% tax on his rental income he will be left with £26,800.

His rental income will use up his entire £33,500 basic-rate band, which means £33,500 of his dividend income will be taxed at 32.5% instead of 7.5%, resulting in additional tax of £8,375. However, because all of his dividend income is now subject to higher-rate tax, this time his £5,000 dividend nil rate band will save him 32.5% tax instead of 7.5% tax, a saving of £1,250.

Overall Warren will be left with £19,675 (£26,800 - £8,375 + £1,250).

If the company had not paid him £33,500 rental income, it would have been left with an extra £27,135 to pay out as dividends and Warren would have been left with £18,316 after paying income tax at 32.5%.

Warren is £1,359 better off by paying himself rental income.

Mortgage Interest

Many company owners who personally own their business premises will also have a mortgage on which they personally pay the interest. These interest payments can be offset against your rental income, effectively making some or all of it 'tax free'.

Note that, although tax relief on mortgage interest for residential property is being reduced (see Chapter 19), mortgages used to buy commercial properties are unaffected.

Most company owners will instinctively realise that it would be foolish not to receive rental income if they also have mortgage interest to pay (or other tax-deductible property expenses). Tax-free rental income has to be better than a taxable dividend!

Example 3 – Higher-rate Taxpayer

Warren has a salary and other income of £11,500, is a higher-rate taxpayer and has tax deductible mortgage interest of £5,000. If he gets the company to pay him rental income of £10,000, he'll have a taxable rental profit of £5,000. After paying income tax at 20% he will be left with £4,000 (£10,000 - £5,000 interest - £1,000 tax).

However, his taxable rental income will use up £5,000 of his basic-rate band which means £5,000 of his dividend income will be taxed at 32.5% instead of 7.5%, resulting in additional tax of £1,250. Overall Warren will be left with £2,750 (£4,000 - £1,250).

If the company had not paid him any rental income, it would have been left with an extra £8,100 to pay out as dividends and Warren would have been left with £5,467, after paying income tax at 32.5%. After paying his interest costs Warren would be left with just £467.

Overall, Warren is £2,283 better off paying himself rental income.

Corporation Tax Relief

To keep things simple in the above examples, I assumed that the company pays 19% corporation tax. However, if your company's current accounting period started *before* April 2017, it will have a slightly higher effective corporation tax rate (see Chapter 1).

For example, a company whose current accounting period runs from January to December 2017 will pay 19.25% corporation tax and thus enjoy 19.25% tax relief on its expenses (including rent).

Thus the examples in this chapter may *underestimate* the attractiveness of rent payments versus dividends.

From 1 April 2020 the corporation tax rate will be reduced to 17%.

Dividends, which are paid out of a company's after-tax profits, will then become a bit more attractive (unless, of course, income tax rates are increased further). Companies will enjoy less corporation tax relief on their rent payments and other expenses.

Summary

The above examples illustrate that it is often more tax efficient to get your company to pay you rental income instead of dividend income. Rental income is most tax efficient to the extent that you have tax deductible costs to offset such as mortgage interest. However, the savings vary considerably from case to case so it is essential to do your own number crunching to find out how much tax can potentially be saved.

Entrepreneurs Relief

Although you may be able to save income tax by paying yourself as much rental income as possible, there is at least one reason why it may be a good idea to get your company to pay you a rent that is lower than the true rental value of your trading premises: to save capital gains tax.

If you sell your business, you may be able to claim Entrepreneurs Relief which means you will pay capital gains tax at just 10%.

Trading premises can also qualify for Entrepreneurs Relief, even if you own them personally. But you cannot claim Entrepreneurs Relief if your company has paid you a full market rent (although rent paid for periods before 6 April 2008 is ignored).

If your company pays you a rent that is lower than the market rent, or if you owned the property before 6 April 2008, then a partial claim for Entrepreneurs Relief can usually be made.

If Entrepreneurs Relief is not available when you dispose of your business premises you will be subject to capital gains tax at the normal rates. Fortunately, however, the CGT rates for assets other than residential property were cut in the March 2016 Budget.

If you're a higher-rate taxpayer you will now pay 20% capital gains tax (previously 28%) and you will pay just 10% to the extent that your basic-rate band is not used up by your income.

So it's possible that, even without Entrepreneurs Relief, company owners will be able to benefit from a 10% tax rate on at least some of their capital gains by making sure they don't have much taxable income in the year they sell their trading premises.

Chapter 24

Pay Yourself Tax-free Interest Income

If your company owes you money you can get it to pay you interest. In some cases the interest will be both a tax deductible expense for the company and tax free in your hands – the best case scenario when it comes to extracting money from your company.

In this situation extracting interest income may be more tax efficient than taking a dividend.

How can interest income be tax free? For starters, interest is not subject to national insurance. As for income tax, since April 2015 there's been a 0% starting rate band for up to £5,000 of savings income.

Since 6 April 2016 there's also a new savings allowance which shelters up to £1,000 of interest income from tax if you're a basic-rate taxpayer and £500 if you're a higher-rate taxpayer (additional-rate taxpayers do not benefit from the savings allowance).

In Chapter 19 we were looking at company owners with income from *other sources*, including interest from investments. In this chapter we're looking at a different type of interest income: interest that comes out of your own company.

The £5,000 Starting Rate Band

Not everyone can benefit from the 0% starting rate. It's designed to benefit those with very low income. Hence the £5,000 starting rate band is reduced if you have any *taxable non-savings income*.

Non-savings income includes income from employment, self-employment, pensions and rental properties. Crucially, it does not include dividend income.

For example, if in 2017/18 you have a salary of £11,500 and no other income apart from dividends, you won't have any taxable non-savings income and can receive £5,000 of tax-free interest.

You may also be able to receive additional tax-free interest thanks to the new savings allowance.

But if you have a salary of £11,500 and rental income of more than £5,000, your rental income will eat up all of your starting rate band, so none of your interest income will be tax-free under the 0% starting rate.

You may, however, be able to receive some tax-free interest thanks to the new savings allowance.

The £5,000 starting rate band is not given on top of the basic-rate band, it's part of it. In other words, if you have £5,000 of interest income your basic-rate band will be reduced by £5,000.

This means some of your dividend income may be pushed into the higher-rate tax bracket.

This may reduce the attractiveness of extracting interest income from your company but may not eliminate the benefit altogether.

The New Savings Allowance

The savings allowance (also known as the savings nil rate band) operates separately from, and in addition to, the starting rate band. This means some company owners will be able to pay themselves up to £6,000 of tax-free interest every year.

The personal savings allowance will be especially useful to company owners who cannot use the starting rate band because they have too much non-savings income, e.g. rental income.

They can typically extract £1,000 (basic-rate taxpayers) or £500 (higher-rate taxpayers) of tax-free interest from their companies.

Lending to Your Company

There are lots of circumstances in which company owners may lend money to their companies. For example, it may be a new company that needs some cash to get started or a well-established company that needs money to buy a major asset.

In some cases company owners lend money to their companies indirectly, for example when a dividend is declared but the cash is not withdrawn immediately, perhaps because the company owner wants to reinvest it to help the business grow.

The Mechanics of Extracting Interest Income

There is no requirement for a director to charge interest on a loan account with their own company but if they do it must not exceed a reasonable commercial rate.

If the company pays more than a commercial rate the excess payment could be treated as salary income and subject to income tax and national insurance.

Interest paid to a director on their loan account will usually be an allowable expense for the company, providing the money is used for business purposes. The interest will therefore provide corporation tax relief.

Although your interest income may ultimately be tax free, the company will have to deduct 20% income tax and pay this to HMRC quarterly, using form CT61 which can be requested online.

If this results in a tax overpayment, the director can reclaim the excess through his self-assessment tax return.

Nevertheless, the additional reporting duties and payments may put some company owners off paying themselves any interest.

The company should also issue you an annual interest certificate.

How Much Tax Can You Save?

This will depend on *how much* and what *type* of income you earn.

Example 1
Basic-Rate Taxpayer, No Taxable Non-Savings Income

Gillian is a company director whose salary and other non-savings income (e.g. rental income) come to £11,500. She has £15,000 of dividend income. She charges her company £5,000 interest for a substantial loan she made to help it buy new machinery. Interest is charged at a commercial rate.

The interest will be a tax deductible business expense, saving the company £950 in corporation tax (£5,000 x 19%). Gillian has no taxable non-savings income so all of her interest income will be tax free, being covered by the £5,000 starting rate band (although the company will initially have to withhold 20% tax and pay this to HMRC).

If instead Gillian had decided to not pay herself interest, the company would have an extra £5,000 of taxable profit. After paying £950 corporation tax there would be an extra £4,050 that could be paid out as dividends taxed at 7.5%, leaving Gillian with £3,746.

The potential tax saving is £1,254.

Example 2
Higher-Rate Taxpayer, No Taxable Non-Savings Income

As before Gillian has £11,500 of salary and other non-savings income and £5,000 of interest from her company. However, this time she has dividend income of £50,000 which means she pays 32.5% tax.

Gillian can enjoy £5,000 of tax-free interest income but because the starting rate band is part of the basic-rate band an additional £5,000 of her dividends will be taxed at 32.5% instead of 7.5%, resulting in additional tax of £1,250. So effectively Gillian receives £3,750 after tax.

If she did not pay herself interest, the company would have an extra £5,000 profit. After paying £950 corporation tax there would be an extra £4,050 to pay out as dividends, leaving her with £2,734 after tax.

So for a higher-rate taxpayer with no taxable non-savings income the potential saving is £1,016 (£3,750 - £2,734).

Example 3
Basic-Rate Taxpayer, No Starting Rate Band Available

This time Gillian has £16,500 of salary and rental income, £5,000 of interest income and £15,000 of dividend income.

Because she has £5,000 of taxable non-savings income (£16,500 - £11,500 personal allowance) she will have no starting rate band available. However, thanks to the new savings allowance, £1,000 of her interest income will be tax free and the rest will be taxed at 20%, leaving her with £4,200.

If Gillian did not pay herself interest, the company would have an extra £5,000 of taxable profit. After paying £950 corporation tax there would be an extra £4,050 that could be paid out as dividends taxed at 7.5%, leaving her with £3,746.

So in this case Gillian is £454 better off paying herself interest. Not only is £1,000 of her interest income tax free, the remaining £4,000 is taxed at just 20% (remember the total combined tax rate on dividend income is now roughly 25% if you are a basic-rate taxpayer).

Example 4
Higher-Rate Taxpayer, No Starting Rate Band Available

This time Gillian has £16,500 of salary and rental income, £5,000 of interest income and £50,000 of dividend income.

Once again she will have no starting rate band available. However, thanks to the new savings allowance, £500 of her interest income will be tax free and the rest will be taxed at 20%, leaving her with £4,100.

An additional £5,000 of her dividend income will be taxed at 32.5% instead of 7.5%, resulting in an additional income tax charge of £1,250. So effectively Gillian ends up with £2,850 after tax.

If instead she had decided to not pay herself interest, the company would have an extra £5,000 of taxable profit. After paying £950 corporation tax there would be an extra £4,050 that could be paid out as dividends, leaving her with £2,734 after tax.

So in this case Gillian is £116 better off paying herself interest.

Corporation Tax Relief

To keep things simple in the above examples, I assumed that the company pays 19% corporation tax. However, if your company's current accounting period started *before* April 2017, it will have a slightly higher effective corporation tax rate (see Chapter 1).

For example, a company whose current accounting period runs from January to December 2017 will pay 19.25% corporation tax and thus enjoy 19.25% tax relief on its expenses (including interest).

Thus the examples in this chapter may *underestimate* the attractiveness of interest payments versus dividends.

From 1 April 2020 the corporation tax rate will be reduced to 17%.

Dividends, which are paid out of a company's after-tax profits, will then become a bit more attractive (unless, of course, income tax rates are increased further). Companies will enjoy less corporation tax relief on interest payments and other expenses.

Summary

Some company owners may be able to save over £1,000 by getting their companies to pay them interest.

The potential tax saving is a lot smaller if there is no starting rate band available, for example if the taxpayer has a significant amount of salary income or rental income.

For many taxpayers the additional tax paperwork will nullify the tax savings.

Finally, it's important to point out that very few small company owners can probably pay themselves as much as £5,000 of interest income because the interest you charge your company must be at a commercial rate.

Chapter 25

Pension Contributions: Better than Dividends

Following the increase in dividend tax rates, some company owners will probably start paying themselves smaller dividends and get their companies to make pension contributions instead.

There are several reasons why pension contributions are attractive:

- Like salaries, company pension contributions enjoy corporation tax relief. In other words, they're a tax deductible business expense.

- When you eventually withdraw money from your pension, 25% can be taken tax free.

- There is no national insurance on pension income.

- Pension income is taxed at the "regular" income tax rates, typically 20% or 40%. By contrast, the combined tax rate (corporation tax and income tax) on dividend income is currently around 25% for basic-rate taxpayers and roughly 45% for higher-rate taxpayers.

- When you start withdrawing money from your pension, you could find yourself in a lower tax bracket than you are now (most retirees are basic-rate taxpayers).

Putting all this together, there's a strong possibility that you will pay tax on your pension income at an effective rate of just 15% (and possibly lower), compared with the 25% or 45% you are currently paying on your dividend income.

There is, of course, a major drawback with pensions: your money is locked away until you are 55 (rising to 57 in 2028). Nevertheless, when you do reach the minimum retirement age, you can now make unlimited withdrawals.

Example – Higher-rate Taxpayer

Lesleyanne is a company owner and a higher-rate taxpayer.

Let's say she is trying to choose between taking an additional £100 of the company's profit as a dividend or getting the company to invest £100 in her self-invested personal pension (SIPP).

With a dividend the company will pay 19% corporation tax, leaving £81 to distribute. After paying income tax at 32.5% Lesleyanne will be left with around £55. The total tax rate will be roughly 45%.

A company pension contribution will enjoy corporation tax relief so the whole £100 will go straight into Lesleyanne's SIPP. Ignoring investment growth (it doesn't affect the outcome), when she eventually withdraws the money from her pension the first £25 will be tax free and the remaining £75 will subject to income tax.

If Lesleyanne is a basic-rate taxpayer when she retires she will pay 20% tax (£15), leaving her with £85. Thus her effective tax rate will be 15%.

If Lesleyanne is a higher-rate taxpayer when she retires (for example, if she ends up with a significant amount of other assets such as buy-to-let properties) she will effectively pay 40% tax on her taxable pension income (£30), leaving her with £70 overall. Thus her effective tax rate will be 30%, which is still better than the 45% currently payable on her dividend income.

It's also possible that some of Lesleyanne's pension withdrawals will be tax free thanks to her income tax personal allowance. In that case her effective tax rate will be 0%!

This example shows that, for company owners who have not already built up significant pension savings, a company pension contribution is an extremely attractive alternative to additional dividend income.

Of course, one must never lose sight of the fact that your pension savings are placed in a locked box until you are at least 55. So a company pension contribution is only an attractive alternative to a dividend if you have already withdrawn enough money from your company to cover your living costs.

In the previous example the company owner got her company to make a pension contribution to avoid the 32.5% tax payable on dividend income. But are company pension contributions worth making if you're a basic-rate taxpayer? Let's find out:

Example – Basic-rate Taxpayer

Poppy is a company owner and a basic-rate taxpayer.

She too is trying to choose between taking £100 of the company's profit as a dividend and a £100 company pension contribution.

With a dividend the company will pay 19% corporation tax, leaving £81 to distribute as a dividend. After paying income tax at 7.5% Poppy will be left with around £75. The total tax rate will be roughly 25%.

With a company pension contribution the whole £100 will go straight into Poppy's SIPP. Ignoring investment growth, when Poppy eventually withdraws the money from her pension the first £25 will be tax free and the remaining £75 will subject to income tax.

Like Lesleyanne, the effective tax rate on her pension income will be:

- *0% if covered by her personal allowance*
- *15% if she is a basic-rate taxpayer*
- *30% if she is a higher-rate taxpayer*

Once again, if Poppy has enough income to cover her living costs, a company pension contribution is an extremely attractive alternative to additional dividend income... unless Poppy ends up wealthier in retirement and becomes a higher-rate taxpayer.

This could happen if, for example, she eventually inherits a significant amount of money and the investment income takes her over the higher-rate threshold.

If she expects to become a higher-rate taxpayer in the future she may be better off taking as much dividend income as she can taxed at just 7.5%, while she can, and investing the surplus funds in an ISA.

Corporation Tax Relief

To keep things simple in the above examples, I assumed that the company pays 19% corporation tax. However, if your company's current accounting period started *before* April 2017, it will have a slightly higher effective corporation tax rate (see Chapter 1).

For example, a company whose current accounting period runs from January to December 2017 will pay 19.25% corporation tax and thus enjoy 19.25% tax relief on its expenses (including pension contributions).

Thus the examples in this chapter may *underestimate* the attractiveness of pension contributions versus dividends.

From 1 April 2020 the corporation tax rate will be reduced to 17%.

Dividends, which are paid out of a company's after-tax profits, will then become a bit more attractive (unless, of course, income tax rates are increased further). Companies will enjoy less corporation tax relief on their pension contributions and other expenses.

Auto-Enrolment

For several years now the Government has been rolling out a system of compulsory pensions called auto-enrolment. Essentially it's an extra tax on employers.

Only employees earning more than £10,000 and aged from 22 to state pension age need to be *automatically* enrolled into a pension. Some older and younger employees and those who earn less than £10,000 also have certain workplace pension rights.

According to the Pension Regulator a company does not have any automatic-enrolment duties when:

- It has just one director, with no other staff

- It has a number of directors, none of whom has an employment contract, with no other staff

- It has a number of directors, only one of whom has an employment contract, with no other staff

A contract of employment does not have to be in writing. However, according to the Pension Regulator, if there is no written contract of employment, or other evidence of an intention to create an employer/worker relationship between the company and the director, it will not argue that an employment contract exists.

If a director does not have an employment contract they are always exempt from automatic enrolment. If a director has a contract of employment and there are other people working for the company with an employment contract, they are not exempt.

Depending on their age and earnings, they may qualify for automatic enrolment but the company can decide whether to automatically enrol them into a pension. However, the director has the right to join a pension scheme at any time and the company cannot refuse to enrol them (although in practice this problem will not arise in most owner-managed companies).

If the company decides not to enrol any employed director who is eligible for automatic enrolment, and it has no other eligible staff, it does not need to set up a pension scheme. However, it will need to make a 'declaration of compliance'.

Chapter 26

Pension Contributions: You or the Company?

In the previous chapter we showed that company pension contributions can be an attractive alternative to dividends.

However, company directors can also make pension contributions *personally*, so a key question is:

"Who should make the contributions: the director or the company?"

Before the increase in dividend tax rates it was often more tax efficient for a small pension contribution to be made by the company director personally.

At present it is often tax efficient in most cases to get your company to make the pension contributions, although this may change in future when the corporation tax rate is reduced further.

Company Owner Pension Contributions

When you make pension contributions *personally* (as opposed to getting your company to make them) the taxman will top up your savings by paying cash directly into your pension. Effectively for every £80 you invest, the taxman will put in an extra £20.

Why £20? Your contributions are treated as having been paid out of income that has already been taxed at the 20% basic rate of income tax.

The company that manages your pension plan – usually an insurance company or SIPP provider – will claim this money for you from the taxman and credit it to your account.

So whatever contribution you make personally, divide it by 0.80 and you'll get the total amount that is invested in your pension pot. This is known as your *gross pension contribution*.

Example

Peter is a company owner who takes most of his income as dividends. He invests £800 in a self-invested personal pension (SIPP). The taxman will top up his pension with £200 of basic-rate tax relief which means he'll have £1,000 in his pension pot:

$$£800/0.80 = £1,000$$

If Peter is a higher-rate taxpayer he can also claim higher-rate tax relief when he completes his tax return. This is given by increasing his basic-rate band by the amount of his gross pension contribution.

Example continued

Peter's gross pension contribution is £1,000 so his basic-rate band will be increased by £1,000. This means £1,000 of his dividend income will be taxed at 7.5% instead of 32.5%, i.e. a 25% saving. Thus, Peter's higher-rate tax relief is:

$$£1,000 \times 25\% = £250$$

In total Peter will enjoy £450 of tax relief (£200 basic-rate relief plus £250 higher-rate tax relief). Peter's total tax relief is 45% of his £1,000 gross pension contribution.

Company Directors with Small Salaries

To obtain tax relief on your pension contributions they have to stay within certain limits:

- **Earnings**. Contributions made by you *personally* must not exceed your 'relevant UK earnings'. Earnings include your salary, bonus and taxable benefits in kind but do NOT include your dividends.

- **The £40,000 Annual Allowance.** Total pension contributions by you and your company must not exceed £40,000 per year, although it is possible to carry forward any unused annual allowance from the three previous tax years. The annual allowance is reduced if your "adjusted income" exceeds £150,000.

For a company director taking the 'optimal' tax-free salary of £8,164, the maximum pension contribution that can be made in 2017/18 is therefore £8,164.

This is the maximum *gross* contribution. The director would personally invest £6,531 (£8,164 x 80%) and the taxman will top this up with £1,633 in basic-rate tax relief for a total gross contribution of £8,164.

For a company director taking a salary of £11,500, the maximum gross pension contribution is £11,500. The director would personally invest £9,200 (£11,500 x 80%) and the taxman will top this up with £2,300 in basic-rate tax relief for a total gross contribution of £11,500.

Directors who want to make bigger pension contributions personally have to pay themselves bigger salaries. However, this is usually not an attractive option because a bigger salary may be subject to both employee's and employer's national insurance (at 12% and 13.8% respectively).

Company Pension Contributions

As a company owner you can also get your company (your employer) to make pension contributions on your behalf. Company pension contributions are always paid *gross* (there is no top up from the taxman) but the company will normally enjoy corporation tax relief on the payment.

For example, a company paying 19% corporation tax can make a pension contribution of £10,000 and enjoy £1,900 tax relief.

Note you do not need a dedicated company pension scheme to make company pension contributions. Most firms that offer SIPPs have special forms that allow your company to pay directly into your pension.

How much can your company contribute? Unlike the contributions that you make personally, the company's contributions are NOT restricted by the size of your salary.

In other words, the company can make a pension contribution that is bigger than your salary.

However, there are other restrictions on company contributions:

- Total pension contributions by you and your company must not exceed annual allowance (typically £40,000), although you can carry forward any unused allowance from the previous three tax years.

- The company may be denied corporation tax relief on any pension contributions made on behalf of directors, if the taxman views them as 'excessive' (see below).

Corporation Tax Relief on Pension Contributions

Unlike the pension contributions that you make personally, tax relief for company pension contributions is not automatic.

Company contributions will only be a tax deductible expense for corporation tax purposes if they are incurred wholly and exclusively for the purposes of the trade.

There is a danger that HMRC will deny corporation tax relief for 'excessive' pension contributions. In practice this is relatively rare.

When determining whether company pension contributions qualify for corporation tax relief, HMRC will look at the total remuneration package of the director. The total package (including salary, pension contributions and other benefits in kind) must not be excessive relative to the work the individual carries out and his or her responsibilities.

Relevant factors may include:

- The number of hours you work, your experience and your level of responsibility in the company.

- The pay of other similar employees in your company and other companies.

- The pay required to recruit someone to take over your duties.

- The company's financial performance.

Extra care may be necessary in the event of a large one-off company pension contribution.

It may be sensible to document the commercial justification (e.g. strong recent financial performance of the company) in the minutes of a directors' board meeting and hold a shareholders' meeting to approve the contribution.

In some cases, when a much larger than normal contribution is made, it may be necessary to spread tax relief over a number of years. These spreading rules will not affect most small companies and only kick in when the excess contributions amount to £500,000 or more.

In conclusion, although the risk that your company will be denied corporation tax relief may be small, it is important to stress that, when it comes to company pension contributions, unlike contributions made by individuals, there is no cast-iron guarantee that the company will enjoy tax relief.

That's why I would recommend speaking to a tax advisor before your company starts making significant contributions.

Pension Contributions – You or the Company?

Using a couple of case studies we will now compare company pension contributions with pension contributions made personally by company owners to see which is most tax efficient.

Case Study 1 – Basic-rate Taxpayer

Eva owns Cassidy Ltd. She is a basic-rate taxpayer and pays herself a small tax-free salary of £8,164 and takes the rest of her income as dividends.

In 2017/18 she decides to make a £1,000 pension contribution. If Cassidy Ltd makes the contribution it can pay £1,000 directly into Eva's SIPP.

If instead Eva pays herself a dividend to fund a pension contribution that she makes personally the company will pay 19% corporation tax leaving Eva with £810.

Eva holds onto £10 and invests £800 in her SIPP. The taxman will add £200 of basic-rate tax relief, leaving her with the same amount in her pension – £1,000.

But that's not the end of the matter: Eva will still have to pay 7.5% tax on her £810 dividend – roughly £60.

Eva is worse of by about £50 (£60 - £10 of saved dividend income).

Thus, if you're a basic-rate taxpayer, for every £1,000 that ends up in your pension you will have to pay an additional 5% in tax.

In this case a company pension contribution is clearly more tax efficient than a contribution made personally by the director.

Other Important Points

If Eva wants more than £8,164 invested in her pension, making the contribution personally will be even more expensive.

She would have to pay herself a bigger salary and this could result in a significant amount of national insurance becoming payable. This is because any pension contribution you make personally cannot exceed your earnings (i.e. salary).

The additional salary would attract 12% employee's national insurance and 13.8% employer's national insurance (unless there is spare employment allowance).

Case Study 2 – Higher-rate Taxpayer

This time we'll assume Eva is a *higher-rate taxpayer* and again wants to make a £1,000 pension contribution.

If Cassidy Ltd makes the contribution it can pay £1,000 directly into Eva's SIPP. Alternatively Eva can pay herself an £810 dividend, hold onto £10 and invest £800 in her SIPP. The taxman will add £200 of basic-rate tax relief, resulting in the same gross pension contribution of £1,000.

Again, that's not the end of the matter. Eva still has to pay income tax on the additional dividend.

With a gross pension contribution of £1,000, Eva's basic-rate band will be increased by £1,000. This means the £810 dividend will be taxed at just 7.5%, not 32.5%, so the tax is roughly £60.

Furthermore, an additional £190 of her other dividend income will also be taxed at 7.5% instead of 32.5%, saving her an extra £48.

All in all a £1,000 pension contribution made by the director is only £2 more expensive than a contribution made by the company:

£60 income tax - £48 higher-rate relief - £10 saved dividend = £2

In this case a company pension contribution is again more tax efficient than a contribution made personally by the director but the difference is tiny.

Because the saving is so small it will probably be other factors that determine whether the company or the individual makes the pension contributions.

The small penalty for making pension contributions personally will be reversed when the corporation tax rate is reduced to 17% – i.e. it may then become slightly more tax efficient to make pension contributions personally if you are a higher-rate taxpayer.

Other Important Points

Note that if Eva wants to enjoy full higher-rate tax relief on a gross pension contribution of £8,164 (i.e. equal to her salary), she must have at least £8,164 of dividend income above the higher-rate threshold (income of at least £53,164 in 2017/18).

If Eva wants to make a pension contribution bigger than £8,164 personally she will have to pay herself a bigger salary and this may result in a significant amount of national insurance becoming payable.

Lifetime ISAs

Those aged 18 to 39 can open a Lifetime ISA which can be used to save for a first home or for retirement.

Up to £4,000 per year can be invested and will receive a 25% Government bonus. So if you put in £4,000, the Government will add £1,000. This is the same as the basic-rate tax relief enjoyed on pension contributions.

It will be possible to continue making contributions up to age 50.

This means you will be able to invest up to £128,000 between age 18 and 50 with a Government bonus of up to £32,000.

Unlike a pension, your savings are not locked up inside a Lifetime ISA. However, if you withdraw money before reaching age 60, for any reason other than to buy your first home, there will be a 25% early withdrawal charge. This will claw back all of the Government bonus, plus an additional 6.25% of the amount you invested.

Lifetime ISA versus Company Pension Contribution

The Lifetime ISA could be an attractive alternative to saving in a pension if you are a basic-rate taxpayer. Like pensions they will attract a top up from the Government but, unlike pensions, ALL the money you take out will be tax free.

For example, let's say a company owner who is a basic-rate taxpayer is trying to decide between a £1,000 company pension contribution and using a dividend to fund a Lifetime ISA contribution.

A £1,000 pension contribution will attract corporation tax relief so the whole £1,000 will go directly into the company owner's pension.

If the same money is used to fund a dividend, the company will pay 19% corporation tax leaving £810 to pay out. After paying 7.5% income tax the company owner will be left with around £750 to invest in a Lifetime ISA. Adding the Government bonus the company owner will end up with £938 in his Lifetime ISA.

However, when the company owner retires all withdrawals from the Lifetime ISA will be tax free, whereas only 25% of the money withdrawn from the pension will be tax free. The rest will be taxed at 20% if he is a basic-rate taxpayer.

If we ignore investment growth to keep the example simple (it doesn't affect the outcome), with a Lifetime ISA the company owner will end up with £938, with a pension he will end up with just £850 after tax.

Thus, if you're a basic-rate taxpayer, your retirement income could be 10.3% higher with a <u>Lifetime ISA</u>!

What about higher-rate taxpayers?

Once again a £1,000 pension contribution will attract corporation tax relief so the whole £1,000 will go directly into the company owner's pension.

If the same money is used to fund a dividend, the company will pay 19% corporation tax leaving £810 to pay out. After paying 32.5% income tax the company owner will be left with £547 to invest in his Lifetime ISA. Adding the Government bonus the company owner will end up with £684 in his Lifetime ISA.

When the company owner retires all withdrawals from the Lifetime ISA will be tax free, whereas only 25% of the money withdrawn from the pension will be tax free. The rest will be taxed at 20% if he is now a basic-rate taxpayer (most retirees end up as basic-rate taxpayers).

Ignoring investment growth again, with a Lifetime ISA the company owner will end up with £684, with a pension he will end up with £850 after tax.

Thus, your retirement income could be 24% higher with a <u>pension</u>.

However, if the company owner is a higher-rate taxpayer when he retires (for example if he has a lot of income from other sources, e.g. rental property) he will end up with £700 from a pension, compared with £684 from a Lifetime ISA. The difference is small and the investment decision will probably be based on other factors.

Summary

- Company pension contributions are currently more tax efficient than contributions made personally by directors.

- The additional saving is very small if the director is a higher-rate taxpayer and will be reversed when the corporation tax rate is reduced to 17%.

- However, if you want to make a pension contribution bigger than your existing company salary it is usually more tax efficient to get the company to make the contribution rather than pay yourself a bigger salary which may have a significant national insurance cost.

- Tax relief for company pension contributions is not automatic – tax relief could be denied if the contributions are viewed as excessive, although this is rare in practice.

- A Lifetime ISA is an attractive alternative to a company pension contribution if you are a basic-rate taxpayer, although you can only invest £4,000 per year and must be under 40 to open one. Pension contributions remain a more attractive alternative if you are a higher-rate taxpayer.

Chapter 27

Putting Property into a Pension

In Chapter 23 we explained that company owners who own their business premises personally can get the company to pay them rent and this may be an attractive alternative to dividends.

Some company owners also use a SIPP or other pension plan to hold their business premises and in this chapter we'll take a look at the benefits and drawbacks of this alternative.

Note that you can put commercial property into a pension but not residential property, so this option is not available to buy-to-let landlords.

Holding business property in a pension has a number of benefits:

- **Tax-free rent**. The rent your company pays into your pension plan is tax free, i.e. there is no income tax payable by you.

- **Corporation tax relief**. The company can still claim the rent as a business expense, saving it corporation tax.

- **No capital gains tax**. When a property held inside a pension is sold there is no capital gains tax payable.

- **Inheritance tax exemption**. Assets held in a pension fall outside your estate for inheritance tax purposes.

Although the ability to roll up rental income tax free inside a pension is enticing, you must never lose sight of the fact that all the money you eventually withdraw from your pension, over and above your 25% tax-free lump sum, will be subject to income tax.

If you are a higher-rate taxpayer at present but expect to be a basic-rate taxpayer when you retire (most retirees end up as basic-rate taxpayers), it's possible the rental income will ultimately be much less heavily taxed by going the pension route.

Similarly, although property held inside a pension can be sold without incurring capital gains tax, when you eventually withdraw the capital gain most of it (75%) will be subject to income tax. If you are a basic-rate taxpayer when you retire you will pay 20% tax and if you are a higher-rate taxpayer you will pay 40% tax.

By contrast, when you sell business premises that you own personally you will be subject to capital gains tax. Commercial property now benefits from the lower 20% CGT rate and it's possible some of the gain will be taxed at just 10% if your basic-rate band isn't used up by your other income. Some of the gain may also be covered by your annual exemption, currently £11,300.

In some cases, as we shall see in Chapter 28, a sale of business premises that you own personally will qualify for Entrepreneurs Relief. If so, a tax rate of 10% may apply to the whole gain, although this will generally not be the case if your company has paid you rent at a full commercial rate.

A property held inside a pension doesn't have to be sold when you retire. If your own business ceases to occupy the property it can be rented out to someone else who will pay rent to your pension which can roll up tax free.

Although property held inside your pension may fall outside your estate for inheritance tax purposes, in most cases the family members that inherit your pension pot will have to pay income tax on any money they subsequently withdraw, typically at 20% or 40%.

By contrast, if you own a business property personally it may qualify for 50% business property relief, i.e. inheritance tax will only be payable on half its value.

Finally, when it comes to tucking away money inside a pension we must never lose sight of the fact that you will not be able to get your hands on any of the money until you are at least 55 (rising to 57 in 2028).

Clearly there are benefits to holding business property inside a pension but it is by no means a 'no brainer'. There are benefits but also drawbacks and each case would have to be decided on its merits with help from a professional.

Funding the Property Purchase

The purchase of a business property by a pension can be funded in several ways.

Typically the company owner will use his or her existing pension savings, topped up with fresh contributions made by the company and/or the company owner personally.

It is also possible for your pension fund to borrow money but only up to 50% of its net assets. For example, if you have pension savings of £100,000 an additional £50,000 can be borrowed.

Some pension providers allow a part share in a property to be acquired by the pension plan, with the balance owned outside the pension.

Several individuals can also pool their pension savings to collectively buy a property.

Transferring Existing Property

If you already own the property you can sell it to your SIPP and this may allow you to release a sizeable amount of cash from your pension savings.

Properties have also been transferred into pensions as *in specie* pension contributions, with the member claiming full income tax relief. Under this method a property worth, say, £100,000 would be transferred into the pension scheme with the pension scheme administrator claiming £25,000 of basic-rate tax relief to add to the member's pension pot and the member himself claiming up to £25,000 of higher-rate tax relief when he submitted his tax return.

In specie contributions are no longer permitted by many pension firms following a recent clamp down by HMRC because of perceived abuse.

Transferring an existing property into a pension is likely to result in capital gains tax becoming payable if the property has risen in value since you bought it.

As stated earlier, commercial property now benefits from the lower 20% CGT rate and some of the gain may be taxed at just 10% and some may be tax-free thanks to the annual exemption. It's unlikely that Entrepreneurs Relief would be available in such cases, however.

A sizeable capital gains tax bill may put off many existing property owners going down the pension route but others may still be tempted by the prospect of receiving a large cash payment out of their pension savings.

The transfer may also result in stamp duty land tax.

VAT may also be payable in certain circumstances but a refund can usually be claimed.

Costs and other Formalities

Not all pension providers deal with property purchases so you may need to transfer your existing pension savings to a specialist provider.

When your property is held inside a pension your company will have to be treated just like any other tenant, with no special favours, which means rent will have to be paid at a full market rate come hell or high water.

If rent is not paid this will be treated as an unauthorised payment by your SIPP and HMRC may levy a charge of 40% on you personally and a charge of up to 40% on the SIPP itself.

Property SIPPs are also much more expensive to run than those that only allow you to invest in traditional 'stocks and shares'.

Initial set up costs include legal fees, surveyor fees, lenders fees and fees to the pension company managing your SIPP.

Fees will have to be paid for regular rent revaluations and a third party property manager may have to be appointed to collect the rent from you.

Chapter 28

Sell Your Business and Pay 10% Tax!

One of the most tax-efficient ways to grow your wealth is to build and then sell several companies during your working life.

This allows you to convert streams of heavily taxed income into low-taxed capital gains.

Many company owners who receive dividends now have a marginal income tax rate of 32.5%. Those with income over £150,000 have a marginal tax rate of 38.1%.

But when you sell a company and receive a cash lump sum, which replaces all of this heavily taxed income, you could end up paying just 10% tax thanks to Entrepreneurs Relief.

At present you can have up to £10 million of capital gains taxed at 10% over your lifetime thanks to this relief. This amount is doubled up in the case of couples.

Although serial entrepreneurs may pay much less tax than other business owners, this lifestyle is not for everyone. However, even if you only own one company it's still a good idea to have a basic understanding of the Entrepreneurs Relief rules in case you do eventually sell your company or wind it up.

With Entrepreneurs Relief there are certain things you need to check and do *before* you sell or wind up your company. Because this generous relief can save a couple up to £2 million in capital gains tax, it's certainly worth knowing what you have to do to protect it!

If you are denied Entrepreneurs Relief you could end up paying capital gains tax at 20% instead of 10% if you are a higher-rate taxpayer. It's also possible that the distributions you receive from your company during a winding up could be treated as dividend income and taxed at up to 38.1%.

Qualifying for Entrepreneurs Relief

Company owners are entitled to Entrepreneurs Relief when they sell shares in the company. The main qualifying criteria are the following:

- The company must be your 'personal company', i.e. you must own at least 5% of the ordinary share capital and voting rights

- You must be an officer or employee of the company

- The company must be a 'trading' company

All three of these requirements must be met for at least one year before the business is sold. It does not matter if the requirements are met in earlier years.

The one-year rule means that you should be wary of incorporating any business within one year of selling it. To qualify for Entrepreneurs Relief you have to own the shares of the newly formed company for at least one year.

You should also be wary of transferring shares in the company to your spouse if a sale is anticipated. Transfers to spouses are exempt from CGT and your spouse can claim Entrepreneurs Relief when the business is sold, providing he or she satisfies the necessary conditions outlined above. The transfer would therefore usually have to be done at least one year before any sale is agreed.

Transfers to spouses were a useful way of increasing Entrepreneurs Relief claims when the lifetime limit was just £1 million. Now that the limit has been raised to £10 million per person most company owners will not need to transfer shares to their spouses to reduce capital gains tax.

However, many company owners transfer shares to their spouses to reduce the income tax payable on dividends (see Chapter 20). If such a transfer were to take place within one year of selling the company, the recipient spouse will not be able to claim Entrepreneurs Relief.

Turning to the three qualifying criteria listed above, most small company owners will have no problem meeting the first two requirements. Company officers include non-executive directors and company secretaries, so you don't even have to work full-time at the company to qualify.

The third requirement could cause headaches for some company owners. HMRC regards the following as non-trading activities:

- Holding investment property
- Holding shares or securities
- Holding surplus cash

If there is substantial non-trading activity you could be denied Entrepreneurs Relief. Unfortunately to the taxman 'substantial' means as little as 20% of the company's:

- Assets
- Turnover
- Expenses
- Profits
- Directors' and employees' time

So, for example, if just 20% of the assets or income of the business are not trading assets or income, you may be denied Entrepreneurs Relief when you sell your business. As a result you may end up paying capital gains tax at 20% instead of 10%.

If your company doesn't own investment property or invest in other companies, the most serious danger is holding too much cash. If the taxman believes the cash is held for non-trading reasons (e.g. to avoid declaring taxable dividends), trading status could be revoked and Entrepreneurs Relief will be taken away.

However, this should not be a problem if you can prove that the cash was required for business purposes, for example as part of a well-documented expansion plan.

Some tax advisors argue that having a large cash balance may not pose a threat to an Entrepreneurs Relief claim if the cash was generated from trading activities and is not 'actively managed' like an investment (i.e. if the cash is left to earn deposit interest only).

However, it's all a bit of a grey area and professional advice is recommended. If the company does have surplus cash it may be necessary to extract it at least one year in advance to prevent the company's trading status being challenged. In such cases you have to weigh up the potential costs and benefits: the benefit being a CGT rate of 10% instead of 20% and the cost being the income tax on any additional dividends.

Selling Property

Many business owners purchase business premises *personally* and rent them back to their company. The good news is Entrepreneurs Relief is available when "associated" assets like these are sold.

The asset will only qualify for Entrepreneurs Relief if you also make a "material disposal" of shares in your company. The stake being disposed of must generally be at least 5% (ordinary shares and voting rights in the case of a company).

It is possible to claim Entrepreneurs Relief on an associated disposal even if the stake in the business is sold or gifted to a family member, for example an adult child. However, there must also be no "share purchase arrangements" in place at the time of disposal. This rule is designed to prevent you from taking back your stake in the business after the property has been sold and Entrepreneurs Relief has been claimed.

To qualify for Entrepreneurs Relief the 'associated' asset must have been in use by the business throughout the period of one year up to the date of the material disposal of shares, or if earlier, the cessation of the business.

For assets acquired since 13 June 2016, the asset must have been held for at least three years to qualify for Entrepreneurs Relief.

Entrepreneurs Relief is also restricted if you've received any payment for the use of the property after 5 April 2008 (for example, if your company has paid you rent to use the property).

Where the property was acquired after 5 April 2008 and a full market rent was received throughout the period of its use in the company's trade, no Entrepreneurs Relief will be available. Where the property was acquired at an earlier date, or rent was charged at a lower rate, there will be a partial restriction in Entrepreneurs Relief.

Winding Up Your Company

It is not always possible to sell your company shares to a third party. Buyers are often fearful of acquiring companies outright for fear of taking on any unknown liabilities. Instead they often prefer to buy the underlying assets (e.g. premises, goodwill, stock and customers).

The disadvantage of an asset sale such as this is the potential double tax charge. Firstly, your company will pay corporation tax on the proceeds, although indexation relief will be available on certain assets such as property. If you then extract the after-tax proceeds a second tax charge may arise.

Providing you meet the qualifying criteria, Entrepreneurs Relief is still available if you wind up your company following an asset sale and extract the cash as a capital distribution.

There are generally two ways to wind up a company:

- Dissolution under the Companies Act
- Voluntary liquidation under the Insolvency Act

With a *dissolution* capital gains tax treatment is only possible if the total distributions are less than £25,000. Where the total distributions exceed £25,000 they are taxed as dividends, possibly at 32.5% or 38.1%.

A *voluntary liquidation*, on the other hand, ensures that payments to shareholders are treated as capital distributions for capital gains tax purposes.

However, voluntary liquidation requires the appointment of a licensed insolvency practitioner with fees running to many thousands of pounds in some cases (the fees may be less if the company's affairs are simple and its main asset is cash).

To qualify for Entrepreneurs Relief the capital distribution must be made within three years of the cessation of trading.

Furthermore, in the 12 months before the cessation of trading the following criteria must be met:

- The company must be your 'personal company', i.e. you must own at least 5% of the ordinary share capital and voting rights

- You must be an officer or employee of the company

- The company must be a 'trading' company

In some cases the existence of a large cash balance (a non-trading asset) may throw in doubt the company owners' ability to claim Entrepreneurs Relief.

It goes without saying that in all cases where a winding up of the company is to be carried out, professional advice should be obtained to ensure the desired tax treatment of the distributions.

New Rules for Wind-Ups

A new anti-avoidance rule applies from 6 April 2016 and means that a distribution made when winding up a company will be taxed as a dividend in some cases. The rule has been introduced to prevent company owners enjoying the much lower capital gains tax rates.

The new rule applies where all of the following conditions are met:

- **Condition A & B**. The individual holds at least 5% of the ordinary share capital and voting rights and the company is a close company

- **Condition C**. Within two years of the distribution the company owner carries on the same or a similar trade or activity to the company being wound up

- **Condition D**. One of the main purposes of the winding up is to reduce income tax, or
The winding up forms part of arrangements, one of the main purposes of which is to reduce income tax

With regards to Condition C, it makes no difference whether you operate as a sole trader or through a partnership or a new company in which you have at least a 5% interest or through a person with whom you are connected (e.g. your spouse or other close relative).

The test is clearly very subjective and it is feared that it could catch many innocent situations, for example where a company owner retires, winds up his company and a year later decides to take on a few clients or do some work for a family member involved in the same trade.

It is also feared that the third test could be applied broadly. For example, HMRC could argue that if a company owner decides not to pay surplus funds out as dividends prior to the winding up, there is as an 'arrangement' to reduce income tax.

HMRC has provided the following examples which are intended to allay these fears and explain when the new rules will apply:

Example 1
Mr A has been the sole shareholder of a company which carries on the trade of landscape gardening for 10 years. Mr A decides to wind up the business and retire. Because he no longer needs a company he liquidates the company and receives a distribution in a winding up. To subsidise his pension, Mr A continues to do a small amount of gardening in his local village.

Conditions A to C are met, because gardening is a similar trade or activity to landscape gardening. However, when viewed as a whole, these arrangements do not appear to have tax as a main purpose. It is natural for Mr A to have wound up his company because it is no longer needed once the trade has ceased. Although Mr A continues to do some gardening, there is no reason why he would need a company for this, and it does not seem that he set the company up, wound it up and then continued a trade all with a view to receive the profits as capital rather than income. In these circumstances, Mr A's distribution in the winding up will continue to be treated as capital.

Example 2
Mrs B is an IT contractor. Whenever she receives a new contract, she sets up a limited company to carry out that contract. When the work is completed and the client has paid, Mrs B winds up the company and receives the profits as capital. Again, conditions A to C are met because Mrs B has a new company which carries on the same or a similar trade to the previously wound up company. Here, though, it looks like there is a main purpose of obtaining a tax advantage. All of the contracts could

have been operated through the same company, and apart from the tax savings it would seem that would have been the most sensible option for Mrs B. Where the distribution from the winding up is made on or after 6 April 2016, in these circumstances the distribution will be treated as a dividend and subject to income tax.

Example 3
Mrs C is an accountant who has operated through a limited company for three years. She decides that the risk involved with running her own business is not worth her effort, and so decides to accept a job at her brother's accountancy firm as an employee. Her brother's firm has been operating for eight years. Mrs C winds up her company and begins life as an employee.

Conditions A to C are met because Mrs C is continuing a similar activity to the trade that was carried on by the company. She is continuing it as an employee of a connected party, triggering Condition C. But looking at the arrangements as a whole it is not reasonable to assume that they have tax advantage as a main purpose, so Condition D will not be met. Mrs C's company was incorporated and wound up for commercial, not tax, reasons; although she works for a connected party it is clear that the other business was not set up to facilitate a tax advantage because it has been operating for some time. In these circumstances, the distribution from the winding up will continue to be treated as capital, absent any other considerations.

HMRC can also use other so-called "Transaction in Securities" rules to attack distributions when a company is wound up. There is uncertainty amongst tax professionals as to how the various anti-avoidance measures will be applied in practice.

Because the new rules cast doubt over how profits distributed on a winding up will be taxed, it may make sense to pay actual dividends over the course of a few tax years, rather than making a single large distribution when you wind up the company.

Adopting a phased approach to the withdrawal of profits from your company may allow you to enjoy the 7.5% tax rate that applies to basic-rate taxpayers, rather than the 32.5% or 38.1% tax rates that apply to higher and additional-rate taxpayers. Adopting this strategy over several tax years could allow a significant amount of cash to be extracted from the company, especially when the amounts taxed at 7.5% can be doubled up in the case of a company owned by a couple.

Chapter 29

Company Cars, Vans and Motoring Costs

Business Mileage

Where you use *your own car* for business journeys, your company can pay you back using the following mileage rates:

	First 10,000 miles	Above 10,000
Cars and vans	45p	25p
Motorbikes	24p	24p
Bicycle	20p	20p

If you take one of your employees in your car on a business journey you can claim an extra 5p per mile.

The above rates are supposed to cover not just your fuel costs but also wear and tear on the vehicle.

The amount will be tax free in your hands and a tax deductible expense for the company.

For example, if in 2017/18 you rack up 5,000 business miles in your own car, your company can pay you £2,250 tax free (5,000 x 0.45). The company can also claim the expense, saving it corporation tax of £428 (£2,250 x 19%).

If your business mileage comes to 12,000 your company can pay you £5,000 tax free (10,000 x 0.45 + 2,000 X 0.25).

Business mileage does not include travel from your home to your permanent place of work.

Using the above mileage rates is a simple way to obtain tax relief for your business journeys, although it is necessary to keep a record of your business journeys (using a log book, for example).

If your company is VAT registered it is also possible to recover the VAT element of your business fuel costs.

The portion of the 45p/25p mileage rate that is for fuel is generally calculated using HMRC's advisory fuel rates:

www.gov.uk/government/publications/advisory-fuel-rates

For example, if your car has a 1600cc petrol engine the rate at the time of writing is 14p per mile and the VAT element would be 2.33p (14p/6). So for each business mile you can recover 2.33p in VAT.

For example, if you drive 1,000 miles on business during the period you can recover £23 of VAT (1,000 x 2.33p).

However, you will have to keep VAT fuel receipts that contain enough VAT to cover the claim you are making. Possibly more trouble than it's worth, unless there is a lot of business mileage.

Some commentators also argue that your company can recover some of the VAT on your other motoring costs (e.g. repairs) in proportion to the car's business use.

Company Cars

You can also get your company to buy a car for your business and private use. The company will be able to claim tax relief on the running costs and capital allowances on the cost of the car.

That's the good news. The bad news is that you will have to pay income tax each year on the benefit in kind and your company will have to pay employer's national insurance. In many cases these charges are high enough to put off most small company owners going down the company car route.

The taxable benefit (the amount added to your income) is calculated by multiplying the manufacturer's list price by a percentage that depends on the car's CO2 emissions and the type of fuel it uses.

The list price is not the same as the price you pay for the car (the list price is probably higher).

For the lowest emission cars the benefit-in-kind percentage is currently 9%, for the highest emission cars it is 37%.

The AA publishes the various taxable percentages here:

www.theaa.com/allaboutcars/companycartax/cartax_exp.html

For example, for a diesel car with CO2 emissions of 119g/km and a list price of £25,000 the benefit-in-kind percentage will be 25% in 2017/18 which means an amount of £6,250 will be added to your taxable income:

$$£25,000 \text{ x } 25\% = £6,250$$

If you are a basic-rate taxpayer you will pay 20% tax (£1,250) and if you are a higher-rate taxpayer you will pay 40% tax (£2,500).

There is no employee's national insurance payable on the benefit in kind.

The taxable percentage generally increases each year. For the above car it will increase from 25% to 27% in 2018/19 and 30% in 2019/20. Thus a basic-rate taxpayer will pay £1,500 tax in 2019/20 and a higher-rate taxpayer will pay £3,000.

Employer's National Insurance

As a company owner you also have take account of the costs your company will pay. The employer's national insurance cost on the above car benefit will be as follows in 2017/18:

$$£25,000 \text{ x } 25\% \text{ x } 13.8\% = £863$$

Employer's national insurance is a tax deductible expense for the business so the cost net of 19% corporation tax relief will be roughly £700.

Private Fuel Costs

If the company pays your private fuel costs there is an additional fuel benefit charge which is £22,600 for 2017/18. The taxable amount is found by multiplying the above fuel benefit charge by the benefit-in-kind percentage. For example, if the benefit-in-kind percentage is 25%, the taxable amount is £5,650 (£22,600 x 25%). This amount is added to your income and taxed.

The company will also pay £780 national insurance (£5,650 x 13.8%).

To avoid these charges company car users can pay for their own fuel and recover the cost of business journeys using the advisory fuel rates. Use of these rates means there is no income tax or employer's national insurance on the amounts paid to the employee.

Cars with Low Emissions

Zero-emission cars (electric cars) used to be exempt from benefit-in-kind charges. This is no longer the case. The benefit-in-kind percentage for 2017/18 is 9%, rising to 13% in 2018/19 and 16% in 2019/20.

However, in 2020/21 these benefit in kind percentages will fall dramatically for some cars. For cars with zero emissions the benefit-in-kind percentage will be just 2%.

Capital Allowances

The company can claim tax relief on the cost of the car in the form of capital allowances. These depend on the car's CO_2 emissions and are currently as follows:

- Over 130g/km   8% per year
- Over 75g/km, up to 130g/km   18% per year
- 75g/km or less   100%

The threshold for the 18% rate will be reduced from 130g/km to 110g/km with effect from 1 April 2018.

The 100% first-year allowance for new low-emission cars has been extended to 31 March 2021, although the qualifying threshold will be reduced from 75g/km to 50g/km from 1 April 2018.

If a loan is taken out to buy the vehicle the interest costs are also an allowable expense, as are running costs such as repairs, insurance and road tax.

VAT cannot be recovered on the purchase price of company cars in the vast majority of cases, although VAT can be recovered on repair costs if the car is used for business purposes.

The 8% and 18% writing down allowances are rather stingy because they're calculated using the 'reducing balance' basis, instead of the more generous 'straight line method'.

For example, if your company buys a car for £10,000 that qualifies for an 18% writing down allowance, it can claim £1,800 in year 1 but only £1,476 in year 2:

$$(£10,000 - £1,800) \times 18\% = £1,476$$

Each year the amount that can be claimed gets smaller, so it takes many years to recover all the tax relief.

Furthermore, unlike sole traders and partnerships, companies cannot claim a balancing allowance when they sell a car for less than its written down value.

For example, if a car with a written down value of £5,000 is sold for just £2,000 a sole trader can claim a balancing allowance of £3,000 in the year the car is sold. Companies cannot do this. A company will have to claim writing down allowances at 8% or 18% on the £3,000 balance, meaning it could take many years to claim all the tax relief.

Leased Cars

If the vehicle is leased the monthly payments are generally a tax deductible expense for the company, although 15% of the payments are not allowable if the car has CO_2 emissions above 130 g/km (110 g/km from April 2018).

Capital allowances cannot be claimed as well.

For cars that have some private use 50% of the VAT on the lease payments can be recovered. All of the VAT for repair and maintenance costs can be recovered.

Company Vans

The cost of vans is usually allowable in full thanks to the annual investment allowance.

Some of the VAT can also be reclaimed to the extent the van is used for business purposes.

Note, vans don't just include Ford Transits and the like. Many double cab pickups are more like 4x4s but qualify as vans for tax purposes.

If the van is used regularly for private purposes the annual benefit-in-kind charge in 2017/18 is £3,230, resulting in income tax of £646 if you're a basic-rate taxpayer and £1,292 if you're a higher-rate taxpayer. There will also be employer's national insurance of £446.

The fuel benefit charge for vans is just £610.

The benefit-in-kind on zero emission (electric) vans is 20% of the normal benefit-in-kind for company vans for 2017/18.

Chapter 30

Mobile Phones

"I turn now to what I regard as one of the greatest scourges of modern life. I refer to the mobile telephone."

With these words former Chancellor of the Exchequer Norman Lamont announced a new tax on mobile phones in his 1991 Budget.

"I hope that, as a result of this measure, restaurants will be quieter and the roads will be safer," he concluded.

His words look rather quaint now, although I'm sure many readers would echo his sentiments!

Fortunately the tax treatment has changed and mobile phones are now a tax-free benefit.

The benefit is limited to one mobile phone per employee, although a second phone may be exempt if private use is insignificant. Phones supplied to family members do not qualify, unless they too are employees.

Also, the contract must be in the company's name.

These days HMRC accepts that smart phones are mobile phones and not computers. Tablets and laptops are excluded. Thus you can get your company to provide you with an iPhone and this will not give rise to a taxable benefit. The company must retain ownership, however.

Part 7

Salary & Dividends: Practical Issues & Dangers

Chapter 31

How to Avoid the Minimum Wage Rules

If you take a small salary from your company (for example, £8,164 or £11,500) there is a danger of falling foul of the national minimum wage (NMW) or the new national living wage (NLW).

Where wages are too low, HMRC will force the company to make up the shortfall. Bigger wage payments may result in bigger national insurance bills for both the company and the director.

There is also a penalty equivalent to 200% of the unpaid wages with a maximum penalty of £20,000 per worker. Those found guilty will also be considered for disqualification from being a company director for up to 15 years.

However, the key point to note about the NMW/NLW is that it only applies to directors who have a contract of employment.

Due to the informal set up in many small companies, there may be some uncertainty as to whether an employment contract exists between the director and the company (employment contracts do not need to be in writing).

However, it is generally accepted amongst the tax profession that if you do not issue yourself with an explicit contract of employment the minimum wage regulations will not apply.

This means you should be able to continue paying yourself a small salary, even if it is less than the national minimum wage or national living wage.

However, risk averse company owners (those worried about potential penalties) should consider paying themselves enough salary to satisfy the minimum wage regulations.

National Living Wage Rates

The new national living wage applies to those aged 25 and over. The rate is currently £7.50 per hour.

If you spend, say, 35 hours per week actively managing your business, the total salary due for 2017/18 will be:

$$35 \times 52 \text{ weeks} \times £7.50 = £13,650$$

Fortunately this is not hugely higher than the optimal salary amounts but will still result in unwelcome national insurance charges.

The national insurance payable on this salary by the director would be £658 and £757 would be payable by the company (£0 if the company has spare employment allowance).

Of course, every case is different and some directors will be able to argue that they spend fewer hours actively managing the business.

Although it may seem that the best strategy is to simply not have a contract of employment, there may be other reasons why having such a contract is important.

Company Owners Who Aren't Directors

It is possible that some family members will be employees of the company but not directors. These individuals are subject to the NMW or NLW for all hours spent working in the business (although directors are exempt with respect to hours spent performing their duties as directors).

However, it is possible that if they only work part time, the salary that must be paid to them will still be within the optimal amounts of £8,164 or £11,500.

Chapter 32

Is My Salary Tax Deductible?

One of the benefits of getting your company to pay you a salary is that the amount will normally be a tax deductible expense and reduce the company's corporation tax bill.

However, it is important to point out that there is no automatic right to corporation tax relief. The amount paid has to be justified by the work carried out for the business and the individual's level of responsibility.

While this may not be an important issue for company owners who work full time in the business and pay themselves a small salary, it may be important if you start paying salaries to other family members, in particular those who only work on a part time basis.

The question of whether your employment income will attract corporation tax relief may also become an issue if you decide to pay yourself a large one-off bonus.

Some of the factors that may determine whether a salary or bonus payment is tax deductible include:

- The number of hours worked in the business

- The individual's legal obligations and responsibilities (e.g. directors' duties)

- The amount of pay received by the company's other employees

- The pay received by employees at other companies performing similar roles

- The company's performance and ability to pay salaries/bonuses.

In the case of large one-off bonus payments made only to the company's directors/shareholders it may be necessary to document the commercial rationale for the payment to show that the payment is justifiable. This can be done in the minutes of a directors' board meeting.

It may also be advisable to record the approval of any bonus in the minutes of a shareholders' meeting.

Chapter 33

Salary vs Dividends: Non-Tax Factors

Most of this guide focuses on choosing the most tax efficient *level* of income and the most tax efficient *mix* of income (i.e. salary versus dividends).

However, when it comes to withdrawing money from your company there are lots of other non-tax factors that may need to be considered.

This chapter provides a short overview of some of the issues but is not definitive.

Cashflow and Working Capital Needs

When deciding how much income you withdraw from your company you must consider the cashflow and working capital requirements of the business.

It would naturally be irresponsible to pay yourself a large bonus or dividend if this affects the company's ability to carry on its business.

If you prefer to retain the cash in your company, it may be possible for a dividend to be declared but not paid out. The dividend can simply be credited to the director's loan account and withdrawn at a later date when it is more convenient.

Income tax will still be payable on any dividends declared but not paid.

Dividends & Company Insolvency

Dividends should not be declared when the company is insolvent or if the payment of those dividends will render the company insolvent.

Dividends that are deemed illegal may have to be repaid, even if this results in the director being made bankrupt or being forced into an individual voluntary arrangement (IVA).

Company's Profitability

The payment of a large salary or bonus will depress the company's profits. This may affect the company's ability to borrow.

Directors Ability to Borrow

If you take a small salary and the rest of your income as dividends there is a possibility that this will affect your ability to borrow money personally.

Some lenders may only be interested in the level of your salary and ignore your dividends, being unfamiliar with this sort of pay structuring.

Other lenders, on the other hand, will look at the complete picture and will look at your recent tax returns and the company's most recent accounts when assessing your ability to repay a loan.

Affect on Share Value

The value of a company is usually based on a multiple of its after-tax profits. A small minority shareholder's stake, however, is often valued according to the dividend history of the company. A consistent or steadily increasing annual dividend may enhance the value of the shares.

Chapter 34

Paying Salaries & Dividends: Profits & Paperwork

Salaries – Real Time Information

Since April 2013 employers have had to report salary payments to HMRC under the Real Time Information (RTI) regime. Under real time information, employers are required to submit a Full Payment Submission (FPS) to HMRC at the same time or before each payment is made to a director or employee.

The idea is to make sure the right amount of tax is paid at the right time. Under the previous system, employers generally only had to report payroll information to HMRC at the end of the year.

Under RTI the directors own salaries could result in additional payroll costs (for example, in small husband and wife companies or 'one man band' companies, where the only salaries paid are those of the directors themselves).

Where the directors receive small salaries, it may be cheaper and easier to register with HMRC as an annual scheme and pay salaries as a single annual lump sum (e.g. in March just before the end of the tax year).

With annual schemes an FPS is only expected in the month of payment and HMRC only has to be paid once a year. However, it is only possible to register as an annual scheme if all employees are paid annually at the same time.

Once a business is registered as an annual scheme, an Employer Payment Summary (EPS) is not required for the 11 months of the tax year where no payments are made to the directors. Schemes not registered as annual schemes have to make monthly submissions, even if no salaries are paid.

An additional problem may arise where directors withdraw cash from their companies and only later decide how these payments are to be treated (for example, as salaries or dividends).

Where the director's loan account is overdrawn, an amount withdrawn and subsequently designated as salary could result in a late filing penalty under RTI.

When directors withdraw money from their companies it is essential to decide up front the nature of the payment (e.g. salary, loan, dividend, reimbursement of expenses) and to have evidence supporting that decision.

For example, where a director borrows money from the company, the terms of the loan should be set out in writing. Withdrawals by directors that cannot be categorised might be treated as earnings by HMRC unless the company can prove otherwise.

Dividends

Distributable Profits

Under the Companies Act a company cannot legally pay a dividend unless it has sufficient distributable profits to cover it.

A company's distributable profits are its accumulated realised profits, less accumulated realised losses. This information can generally be found in the company's most recent annual accounts.

It is not necessary for the company to actually make a profit in the year the dividend is paid, as long as there are sufficient accumulated profits (after tax) from previous years.

If the distributable profits are not big enough to cover the dividend it may be necessary to prepare interim management accounts to justify the payment. A revaluation of an investment property is not a realised profit.

Before paying any dividends it is probably wise to speak to your accountant to check whether the company does indeed have sufficient distributable profits.

It may also be wise to check whether a loss has been realised since the last accounts were drawn up and whether any dividend will cause cash flow problems for the company.

In general, it is wise to be conservative and keep dividends to a reasonable level.

If the company does not have sufficient distributable profits to cover its dividend payments, the dividends will be illegal and the shareholder will be liable to repay the company. If not repaid it could be treated as a loan, resulting in a 32.5% section 455 charge.

Dividend Formalities & Paperwork

It is possible that HMRC will try to tax dividends as employment income. To help avoid any such challenge it is essential to ensure that dividends are properly declared and you have the supporting paperwork to prove it.

This includes:

- Holding a directors' board meeting to recommend the dividend payment (with printed minutes to prove the meeting took place)

- Holding a general meeting of the company's members (i.e. shareholders) to approve the dividend payment (with printed minutes to prove the meeting took place).

- Issuing a dividend voucher to each shareholder.

See the Appendix for sample documentation.

Some commentators also argue that it is not advisable to declare dividends monthly because this will look more like salary income, especially if the above formalities are neglected.

A better alternative would be an infrequent dividend credited to the director's loan account which can then be drawn down throughout the year.

Paying a dividend towards the end of the tax year, when it may be easier to work out how much income tax will be payable, is possibly best in timing terms. If a dividend is paid at the beginning of the year and income from other sources (e.g. rental income) turns out to be higher than expected, the company owner could end up paying tax at a higher rate on his dividend income.

Interim versus Final Dividends

A final dividend must be recommended by the directors and endorsed by a shareholders meeting. For tax purposes the dividend is treated as paid on that date (unless a later date is specified).

Interim dividends can be authorised at the discretion of directors and are recognised for tax purposes only when they are paid, for example by crediting the director's loan account.

Chapter 35

Dividends Taxed as Earnings

Recent tax cases demonstrate the potential danger that dividends paid to a director/shareholder may in some circumstances be vulnerable to a national insurance liability and possibly a full PAYE charge.

It remains to be seen how HMRC will choose to use these decisions in the context of family companies:

P A Holdings

PA Holdings switched from a conventional bonus arrangement to a more intricate structure whereby an employee benefit trust was funded by the company, which in turn awarded preference shares to employees. These preference shares duly paid a dividend after which they were redeemed.

The company and its employees argued that the dividends should be taxed as dividends using dividend tax rates and without any PAYE or national insurance implications.

By contrast, HMRC took the view that the dividends simply amounted to earnings and that the normal PAYE and national insurance payments should have been deducted from them and accounted for to HMRC.

The Court of Appeal overturned the decisions of the First Tier Tribunal and the Upper Tribunal and decided that the dividends were indeed earnings for employment and should therefore suffer deductions of income tax at source through PAYE. Both employers and employees national insurance deductions should also have been made.

PA Holdings initially decided to appeal to the Supreme Court but later threw in the towel. This led to fears that HMRC could attack director/shareholders who take most of their income as dividends.

Many tax advisers argue that the aggressive tax planning undertaken by PA Holdings (trying to change bonuses into dividends for a large chunk of employees) is entirely different to the profit extraction model of most small companies.

In other words, most director/shareholders should be able to continue paying themselves small salaries and taking the rest of their income as dividends with limited risk of challenge from HMRC.

Uniplex (UK) Ltd

Uniplex was sold a scheme aimed at giving employees dividend income instead of remuneration, issuing different classes of share to each employee. This type of arrangement is generally known as alphabet shares.

The scheme failed as it was not implemented as planned. However, the First Tier Tribunal judge added that the scheme, even if implemented correctly, might still have failed.

Stewart Fraser Ltd

This case involved a write off of loans by a close company to an employee shareholder. The loan write offs were treated as distributions taxable on the employee. HMRC successfully argued that national insurance liabilities were payable by the company on the loan write offs.

Practical Implications

The practical implications relate to the boundary between normal dividend payments and those which under the PA Holdings/Uniplex/Stewart Fraser case principles would be treated as employment earnings and hence attract income tax and national insurance deductions through PAYE. For instance in PA Holdings the First Tier Tribunal said:

"if something is paid out as a distribution by a company to an investing shareholder then the issue of derivation may arise if the shareholder is also an employee. The facts may show that the derivation of a dividend

from a share may not be related to earnings because the acquisition and ownership of the share was not related to earnings or more generally to the status of the individual as an employee of the company".

In Uniplex, the First Tier Tribunal said:

"The PA Holdings case is authority for the proposition that payments from a party other than the employer can be from an employee's employment" and *"It may well have still been the case that the full amount would have been taxable because employees had given no consideration for the payment other than their services".*

Summary

Dividends paid to an employee-shareholder may in some circumstances be vulnerable to a national insurance liability, and possibly to a full PAYE charge. It remains to be seen how HMRC will choose to use these decisions in the context of family companies and remuneration planning generally.

Dividends from certain alphabet share arrangements, that allow profits to be shared in a way that relates to the amount of work carried out in the business, are at risk of being taxed as employment income.

Most at risk are shares that have no capital or voting rights other than a right to dividend income.

Alphabet share arrangements could also fall foul of the settlements legislation if they are used to divert dividend income to another person.

Chapter 36

Small Salary, Big Dividends: Potential Dangers

It is quite common practice for company owners to pay themselves a small salary and take the rest of their income as dividends. Many accountants have been recommending this strategy for years.

However, it is important to point out that some tax advisors are cautious about certain aspects of this tax planning technique, especially in light of recent court decisions like *PA Holdings*, where the Court of Appeal decided that certain dividends should be subject to PAYE and national insurance (see Chapter 35).

There is a fear that cases like this will create a wide precedent for any employer that pays dividends to its staff. It is difficult to quantify the potential danger, however, because a lot depends on HMRC's willingness to act. The most vulnerable, arguably, are those that use tax planning techniques that HMRC may view as aggressive, including possibly:

- Large scale contrived arrangements where dividends are created for tax avoidance purposes (as in *PA Holdings*).

- Directors' loans that are written off and taxed as dividends.

- Dividend waivers that are used to divert income to other shareholders, for example where a director waives his own dividends so that his wife can receive more income. HMRC recently succeeded in challenging dividend waivers in the case of *Donovan & McLaren v HMRC*.

- Certain 'Alphabet' share arrangements, where different classes of shares (A, B, C etc) have no substantive rights other than to dividends. These arrangements are often used to substitute dividends for bonuses.

- Situations where previous salaries have been reduced in favour of dividends.

The sixty-four thousand dollar question is: where does this leave the average small company owner taking a small salary and the rest of his income as dividends?

At the time of writing it would appear that most small companies are not under attack but this state of affairs could change at any time. The small salary/big dividend tax planning technique does not produce *guaranteed* tax savings. There is a danger, no matter how small, that HMRC may try to tax your dividends as earnings, if not now then at some point in the future.

Also, with regards to the last point in the above list, please note that some (more conservative) tax advisors argue that if you are currently taking a salary that is larger than the 'optimal' amounts listed in Chapter 7 you should not reduce it.

Other tax advisors recommend taking a salary slightly larger than the 'optimal' amounts, so that at least some income tax and national insurance is paid by the director.

Chapter 37

Personal Service Companies

If your company is classed as a personal service company, many of the tax planning opportunities available to other company owners may not be available, for example, the ability to take dividends that are free from national insurance.

Personal service companies often have to operate the infamous 'IR35' regime which means the company may be forced to calculate a notional salary for the director/shareholder.

This deemed income will be subject to PAYE and national insurance.

Essentially, HMRC may ignore the company set up and treat most of the company's income as employment income.

Which Companies Are Affected by IR35?

This is where it all becomes a bit of a grey area (which is why professional advice is essential!)

A personal service company is, generally speaking, a firm that receives all or most of its income from services provided by the director/shareholder.

Often the work will be carried out for just one client, often for a long period of time, and the client will probably only want the personal services of the company owner (hence IR35 often applies to 'one man band' companies).

Essentially HMRC is looking for cases of 'disguised employment'. In other words, ignoring the fact that there is an intermediary company, the relationship is more like that between an employer and employee rather than the kind of relationship that exists between independent self-employed business owners and their clients.

Where such 'disguised employment' exists, the company must apply the IR35 regime to the payments received from that client – effectively treating most of those payments as if they were salary paid to the director/shareholder.

A typical situation which might be caught under the IR35 rules is where the individual resigns as an employee and then goes back to the same job but working through a company.

However, it's all very subjective with a long line of legal cases adding to the confusion.

Personal service companies can be found in many different business sectors: the most cited example is IT consultants.

They also came under the media spotlight in recent times when it was disclosed that some BBC presenters had been operating as 'freelancers' via personal service companies, when many would argue that they are in fact nothing but employees of the BBC.

Recent Changes

In 2015 the Government published a discussion document exploring new ideas, including a proposal that the client engaging the services of a worker providing services through their own limited company should be responsible for deciding whether the IR35 legislation applies and responsible for deducting tax and national insurance.

In the March 2016 Budget it was announced that this approach will be followed by public sector bodies. From April 2017, where a public sector body engages a worker providing services through their own limited company, it will be responsible for determining whether the IR35 rules should apply and for paying the right tax.

There was no mention of a wider application to the private sector use of personal service companies or reform of IR35. However, some tax commentators believe that it is only a matter of time before similar rules are applied to private sector employers.

HMRC's IR35 Digital Tool

HMRC recently launched an online tool to help individuals assess whether the intermediaries legislation applies to any particular engagement:

www.tax.service.gov.uk/check-employment-status-for-tax/setup

It has been widely panned by the experts for being too strict in its assessments.

A key question is *"Has the worker's business arranged for someone else (a substitute) to do the work instead of them during this engagement?"*

If you don't have the right to send someone as a replacement, it would appear there is little chance of the online tool treating you as outside IR35.

Personal service companies and IR35 are beyond the scope of this guide.

Part 8

More Tax Planning Ideas

Chapter 38

How to Pay Less CGT by Postponing Dividends

The main capital gains tax rates were reduced in April 2016:

- From 18% to 10% Basic rate taxpayers
- From 28% to 20% Higher rate taxpayers

Sadly, the 18% and 28% rates still apply to gains arising on disposals of *residential* property.

Where the individual is entitled to Entrepreneurs Relief, the gain is taxed at 10%. Entrepreneurs Relief is generally only available when you sell or wind up a business. In all other cases, the amount of capital gains tax you pay depends on how much income you have earned during the tax year.

In the absence of Entrepreneurs Relief, the maximum amount of capital gains that you can have taxed at 10% or 18% during the current tax year is £33,500. This is the amount of the basic-rate tax band for 2017/18.

Basic-rate taxpayers pay 10% less capital gains tax than higher-rate taxpayers. This means the basic-rate tax band can save each person £3,350 in capital gains tax this year: £33,500 x 10% = £3,350.

Postponing Dividends

If you expect to realise a large capital gain, for example by disposing of a buy-to-let property, you may be able to save quite a lot of tax by making sure the disposal takes place during a tax year in which your taxable income is quite low.

In this respect, company owners can manipulate their incomes more easily than regular employees, sole traders or business partners. The company itself can keep trading and generating profits but the company owner can make sure very little of these profits are extracted and taxed in his or her hands.

Example

Richard, a company owner, sells a buy-to-let property, realising a gain of £50,000 after deducting all buying and selling costs. Deducting his annual CGT exemption of £11,300 leaves a taxable gain of £38,700.

Richard hasn't paid himself any dividends during the current tax year and decides to postpone paying any so that £33,500 of his capital gain is taxed at 18%. The remaining £5,200 will be taxed at 28%. This simple piece of tax planning saves Richard £3,350 in capital gains tax.

Note that Richard can still pay himself a tax-free salary of up to £11,500 to utilise his income tax personal allowance. The income tax personal allowance does not interfere with the capital gains tax calculation. (In practice he may be better off paying himself a slightly smaller salary of £8,164 and a tax-free dividend of £3,336 if his company doesn't have any spare employment allowance.)

Limitations

Although postponing dividends could help you pay less capital gains tax, it's probably not worth doing this unless you can withdraw the postponed dividends in a future tax year and pay no more than 7.5% tax. If you take a bigger dividend in a later tax year, and end up paying 32.5% income tax, you may end up worse off overall.

Remember too that the tax-free dividend allowance is being reduced from £5,000 to £2,000 in 2018/19.

Example continued

In the above example Richard postponed taking a dividend of £33,500 to free up his basic-rate band and pay 18% capital gains tax.

If during 2018/19 he takes an additional dividend of £33,500, on top off his usual salary and maximum dividend taxed at 7.5%, he will pay additional income tax of £10,888 (£33,500 x 32.5%). However, if he had taken that income in 2017/18 he would have paid income tax of £2,138 – so he ends up paying £8,750 more income tax.

He saved £3,350 in capital gains tax in 2017/18 but pays an additional £8,750 in income tax in 2018/19. Overall Richard is £5,400 worse off.

Chapter 39

Emigrating to Save Tax

Possibly the most drastic step you can take to save tax is leave the country!

By becoming non-resident you may be able to avoid both capital gains tax (when you sell your company) and income tax (if you want to withdraw big dividends).

Capital Gains Tax

In the past it was possible to go and live in certain countries for just one year and completely avoid paying capital gains tax.

This was a fantastic loophole, especially when capital gains tax was levied at rates of up to 40%.

Unfortunately that loophole was closed and most UK taxpayers who move abroad temporarily to avoid capital gains tax will be taxed when they return, if the period of non residence lasts for five years or less. (This is a change from the previous anti-avoidance rule which applied if there were fewer than five complete tax years between the year of departure and the year of return.)

With a capital gains tax rate of just 10% applying to many company sales (where Entrepreneurs' Relief applies), many company owners would be unwilling to exile themselves from the UK for five years just to increase their bank accounts by 10%.

Moving abroad is an expensive and time-consuming business and these costs would eat into your tax savings.

Of course, if you plan to emigrate one day anyway, this is all academic. You may be able to live in the country of your dreams **and** avoid paying tax at the same time.

Income Tax

Where a company has built up significant distributable profits it has been possible in the past to withdraw these profits as tax-free dividends during a short period of non-residence.

This tax planning opportunity is no longer available following the introduction of some anti-avoidance rules.

Income from "closely controlled companies" (most small companies) will be taxed if the recipient becomes UK resident again after a temporary period of non residence of five years or less.

This anti-avoidance rule does not apply to dividends paid out of "post-departure" profits, ie profits built up while you are non-resident.

It is not meant to apply to employment and self-employment earnings or regular investment income, eg dividends from stock market companies and bank interest.

Furthermore, the anti-avoidance rule will only apply where an individual has been resident in four or more of the seven tax years prior to the tax year in which they become non-resident.

While it may no longer be possible to avoid income tax by becoming non-resident for a short period, this tax planning strategy may still work for genuine emigrants who decide to leave the UK permanently.

Professional advice should be obtained before attempting to become non-resident to reduce UK taxes.

Statutory Residence Test

So how do you become non-resident?

A statutory residence test has been in operation since 6 April 2013. This test is supposed to make it a lot easier to determine your residence status and hence where you stand when it comes to paying UK tax. Whether it will achieve this aim remains to be seen.

Automatic Overseas Tests

You start with the automatic overseas tests. You will be automatically *non-resident* for the tax year if you meet *any* of the following tests:

- You spend fewer than 16 days in the UK during the tax year. This test is used if you were UK resident in *any* of the previous 3 tax years.

- You spend fewer than 46 days in the UK during the tax year. This test is used if you were UK resident in *none* of the previous three tax years.

- If you work sufficient hours overseas (generally 35 hours or more per week on average) without a significant break, and during the tax year:

  ➢ You spend fewer than 91 days in the UK, and
  ➢ You spend fewer than 31 days working in the UK (a work day means more than three hours work).

If you do not meet any of these automatic overseas tests, you should move onto the 'automatic UK tests'.

Automatic UK Tests

You will be automatically *UK resident* for the tax year if you meet *any* of the following tests:

- You spend 183 days or more in the UK during the tax year.

- You have a home in the UK and are present in that home on 30 or more days during the tax year. This test only applies if you do not have an overseas home or, if you do have an overseas home, you are present in that home on fewer than 30 days during the tax year.

- You work full time in the UK for any period of 365 days (all or part of which falls into the tax year) with no significant break.

If any of the automatic UK tests apply to you for a particular tax year and none of the automatic overseas tests apply, you are UK resident for tax purposes for that tax year.

If you do not meet any of the automatic overseas tests and do not meet any of the automatic UK tests you have to use the sufficient ties test to determine your residence status for the tax year.

Sufficient Ties Test

This test takes into account your UK ties and the number of days you spend in the UK. The more ties you have, the more likely it is that you will be UK resident for tax purposes:

- **Family tie** – your spouse or common-law partner (unless separated) or children under 18 (with some exceptions) are UK resident.

- **Accommodation tie** – you have a place to live in the UK that is available for a continuous period of 91 days or more during the tax year. You don't have to own the property but must spend at least one night there during the tax year or, if it is the home of a close relative, you must spend at least 16 nights in it to have an accommodation tie.

- **Work tie** – you do more than three hours work a day in the UK for a total of at least 40 days. Includes employment and self-employment.

- **90-day tie** – you have spent more than 90 days in the UK in either or both of the previous two tax years.

- **Country tie** – the UK is the country in which you were present for the greatest number of days during the tax year. This tie only applies if you were UK resident in any of the previous three tax years.

These ties are then combined with days spent in the UK to determine your residence status.

The scoring is different for people who have recently left the UK (i.e. were UK resident in any of the previous three tax years) and those who have recently arrived (i.e. were not resident in any of the previous three tax years).

UK Resident in Any of Previous 3 Tax Years – Leavers

UK ties are combined with days spent in the UK as follows:

Days in UK	Residence status
Fewer than 16 days	Always non-resident
16 – 45 days	UK Resident if 4 or more ties
46 – 90 days	UK Resident if 3 or more ties
91 – 120 days	UK Resident if 2 or more ties
121-182 days	UK Resident if 1 or more ties
183 days or more	Always UK resident

Not Resident in All 3 Previous Tax Years – Arrivers

UK ties are combined with days spent in the UK as follows:

Days in UK	Resident Status
Fewer than 16 days	Always non-resident
16 – 45 days	Always non-resident
46 – 90 days	UK resident if all 4 ties
91 – 120 days	UK resident if 3 or more ties
121-182 days	UK resident if 2 or more ties
183 days or more	Always UK resident

Further Information

Finally, please note that many of the terms used in this chapter have complex definitions and there is more to the statutory residence test than can be covered in just a few pages.

For more information see the Taxcafe guides:

- *Tax Planning for Non-Residents & Non Doms.*
- *Tax-free Capital Gains*

Appendix

Sample Dividend Documentation

1. Director's Board Meeting Minute

BOARD MINUTE

Minutes of a Meeting of Directors of Standard Ltd held at 100 London Road, Newtown, ZZ10 1AA on 31st March 2018.

Present: Mr A B Crown – Director
            Mrs D E Crown – Director
            Mr E F Bloodaxe – Director

In attendance: Mr H Godwinson – Company Secretary

Motions:
1) It was recommended that the company pay a dividend of £2.50 per ordinary share out of the profits for the year ended 31st December 2017, to be paid on 1st April 2018.
2) The directors noted the company's excellent trading results for the year ended 31st December 2017 with satisfaction.
3) No other motions.

Signed _____   Date _____
       (Mr A B Crown)

Notes (Not Part of the Minute)
The minutes of a directors' board meeting should:
  a) *Indicate the persons present.*
  b) *Include sufficient information to describe how directors reasonably came to reasonable decisions.*
  c) *Include details of any conflicts of interest or abstainment from voting.*
  d) *Be signed by a director present at the meeting.*
  e) *Be retained with the company's statutory records.*

Regarding point (a) above, a quorum may need to be present for the meeting to be valid. This depends on the company's own constitution as set out in its Articles of Association.

2. Member's General Meeting Minute

GENERAL MEETING OF MEMBERS

Minutes of an Extraordinary General Meeting of the Ordinary Shareholders of Standard Ltd held at 100 London Road, Newtown, ZZ10 1AA on 31st March 2018.

Present: Mr A B Crown – Ordinary shareholder
            Mrs D E Crown – Ordinary Shareholder
            Mr E F Bloodaxe – Ordinary Shareholder

In attendance: Mr H Godwinson – Company Secretary

Motions:
1) The members, all being present, agreed to accept the short notice period for the meeting.
2) The members approved the recommendation of the directors that the company pay a dividend of £2.50 per ordinary share for the year ended 31st December 2017. Payment to be made on 1st April 2018.
3) No other motions.

Signed _____   Date _____
       (Mr A B Crown)

3. Dividend Confirmation/Voucher

Dividend Confirmation

Standard Limited
100 London Road, Newtown, ZZ10 1AA

Ordinary shares of £1 each

Mr A B Crown   1st April 2018
1 Viking Crescent
York
Y1 1AA

Payment of the final dividend in respect of the year ended 31st December 2017, at the rate of £2.50 per share on the ordinary Shares registered in your name on 31st March 2018 is enclosed herewith.

H. Godwinson, Company Secretary

Shareholding	*Dividend Payable*	*Payment Number*
10,000	£25,000.00	11

This dividend confirmation should be kept with your tax records.

Lightning Source UK Ltd.
Milton Keynes UK
UKOW01f1024040717
304603UK00001B/31/P